To Mary —
Thanks for all
your leadership!
Bill Huebsch

GROWING FAITH
PROJECT

Facilitator's Guide

Bill Huebsch

Quotations from the *Catechism of the Catholic Church* are taken from the English translation for the United States of America, ©1994, United States Catholic Conference, Inc.

The Scripture passages contained in this work are from the New Revised Standard Version (NRSV) of the Bible, Catholic Editions. ©1989 by the Division of Christian Education of the National Council of Churches of Christ in the USA. All rights reserved.

The passages from Vatican II quoted in this work are from *Vatican Council II*, general editor, Austin Flannery OP (Northport, NY: Costello Publishing Company, 1996).

The illustration of St. Stephen in booklet #22 was inspired by an image from Monastery Icons. Geneva, NE, ©1985.

Twenty-Third Publications
A Division of Bayard
185 Willow Street
Mystic, CT 06355
800-321-0411
www.twentythirdpublications.com
Also distributed by Harcourt Religion Publishers.

ISBN: 1-58595-400-4

Dedication

The *Growing Faith Project* is dedicated to the leaders in the church whose vision has led us to this moment:

The men and women working in the church around the world
    both at the present time and in the past
    whether paid or volunteer
        in households
        parishes and schools
        universities and colleges
        diocesan and national offices
        and publishing companies
who are committed to helping adults and young adults
        grow closer to Christ
        understand their faith
        worship with awe
        and live accordingly.

Acknowledgments

The *Growing Faith Project* is the work of many hands.

The team at Twenty-Third Publications who helped develop the concept and framework and people who prepared the publication.

Pascal Ruffenach	Dan Connors
Gwen Costello	Andrea Carey
Mary Carol Kendzia	Casey Cyr
Dan Smart	Rob Veal
Alison Berger	Holly Bewlay

The team at Harcourt Religion Publishers who helped develop the design and format
Diane Lampitt
Cassie Nielsen
Sabrina Manguson
Melissa Wurzel

The team in Minnesota who created and developed the original product ideas
Mark Hakomaki, illustrator
Tom Stukel, designer

The general editor
Sr. Maureen Shaughnessy, SC

The parishes who allowed us to test the *Growing Faith Project* with their folks and the many parishioners who gave us feedback and helpful suggestions.

Table of Contents

Appendices

Introduction

"We've been meaning to do this for a long time," one parish religious education director told me. She was talking about bringing adults into the learning circle of her parish.

"Catechesis for adults," the *General Directory for Catechesis* tells us in article 59, "must be considered the chief form of catechesis. All other forms, which are indeed always necessary, are in some way oriented to it." Is this true in your parish?

All of us who work in parish ministry today want to do a better job of reaching adults, of offering them faith formation. We attend conferences and read excellent resources. We talk among ourselves in the hallways and cloak rooms of diocesan meetings. We plan and study and invite and cajole—and sometimes even plot—to find ways to interest adults and help them grow in their faith.

We have learned a few things over the years.

First, adult formation is a two-step process. Pope John Paul II has made a tremendous contribution to our ministry by articulating so clearly that the "first step" for most adults will not be actual instruction in the faith but conversion to Jesus Christ. Within our parish communities, many if not most adults have not turned their hearts to Christ, have not "put on Christ like a garment," as St. Paul suggests. This lack of conversion produces a lack of real heart for the faith. A lack of enthusiasm. Even a lackluster presence in the Sunday Assembly, or no presence there at all.

Again, the "first step" isn't instruction in the faith, but turning our hearts to Christ.

Evangelization

In the Catholic Church today we call the process of introducing folks to Christ "evangelization." For many Catholics, this is a new and difficult term. To many it suggests the television-based ministries popular among evangelical Christians. In Catholic teaching, however, the term evangelization has a meaning different from the one evangelical Christians give it. Catholics believe we cannot know Christ without at the same time knowing and being part of the body of Christ. He is the head of the body which is the church. Knowing Christ is an essential part of being Catholic: participating at Mass, celebrating the sacraments, working for justice and peace, following the precepts of the church, learning from the pastoral leaders of the church, and developing mature, adult faith within a community.

Catechesis

The second step to growing in faith is to study it! As we just said, to know Christ is to know the church. Because of this, studying our faith is one of the ways we come to know Christ better.

That's where *Growing Faith* comes in. Here at last is a product designed for the youth, young adults, and adults of every age and situation in today's church. It's beautiful in design, easy to use, easy to facilitate, and absolutely Catholic!

Growing Faith is designed to support the journey of faith so many Catholics are making today. When used from the first booklet to the last, it provides a systematic and comprehensive presentation of the Catholic faith. Whether you use it in groups or as individuals, you will find the beauty and deep meaning of our faith expressed in down-to-earth language, with illustrations that touch the heart.

Each component booklet opens up one important dimension of our faith. Every new insight about your faith, every reflection that stays in your mind afterward, each line of the text or memory of the artwork, is a gift.

On page 4 is a beautiful opening prayer that can be used alone or with a group. Music for a gathering song and a dismissal song, written by Tom Kendzia, is included on the PowerPoint CD-ROM accompanying this Guide; the words and music to these songs are found on pages 6–9. Sing it or listen to it as you begin your prayerful journey of faith.

Our Catholic faith is rooted in the deepest desires of the human heart: to know God and be with God, to know each other and be with each other. Keep this truth in mind as you enter into this process.

Let Us Pray

Before beginning your study, pause for a moment of silence to collect your thoughts. Bring to mind the spirit of those who are with you or whom you love, and ask the Spirit of Life to be your guide.

If you wish, you can pray the words of Abide, O Spirit of Life, found on the next page. Or you can play the Gathering Song from *Lead Us to the Water*, which can be found on the CD-ROM that accompanies this book. (The music for this song is found on pages 6–7.)

When you finish, open the *Growing Faith* booklet and begin with reverence.

Then as you conclude your work for today, use Be Love: The Prayer of Blessed John XXIII as your closing prayer (see page 5). Or you can play the Dismissal Song from *Lead Us to the Water*, also on the CD-ROM (the music for this song is on pages 8–9). These songs may be played on either a CD player, or on your laptop computer if you are set up for PowerPoint.

Abide, O Spirit of Life

Text: adaptation by Bill Huebsch © 2004. This prayer may have been composed by St. Isidore of Seville, for use during a council held there in 619 and again later in 633. It was used before each session of Vatican I in 1869-70, and it was used before each session of Vatican II in 1962-1965.

Leader	We stand firm, here before you, With our weakness and longing for you. We are bound to love one another. Abide, O Spirit of life!
Refrain	Let peace fill our hearts, Let love fill our minds. Make us loving disciples of Christ. May we all be one, May we all be yours, Abide, O Spirit of Life!
Leader	We ask you to guide all our actions And to show the path we should walk. We desire to know what will please you. Abide, O Spirit of life!

All pray the above refrain

Leader	May you be our sole inspiration, May you see whatever we do, May we act in your name forever. Abide, O Spirit of life!

All pray the above refrain

Leader	May we walk together in justice. Teach us wisdom, unite all our hearts. May your grace be here now to guide us. Abide, O Spirit of life!

All pray the above refrain

Leader	United in your name forever, May our work reflect your desires. May your mercy and love always fill us. Abide, O Spirit of life!

All pray the above refrain

Be Life!

The Prayer of Blessed John XXIII

Text: adaptation by Bill Huebsch © 2004. Adapted from the prayer at the conclusion of the pope's opening speech at Vatican II. This was Blessed John XXIII's prayer for the church, the world, and the council then beginning.

Leader
Be love! Almighty God!
In you we place our confidence,
not trusting in our strength.
Be love! All Loving God!
Look down on us your church,
and send the light of grace!

Refrain
Be love,
Be power,
Be glory for ever and ever!

Leader
Be love! O Holy Spirit,
guide us in our decisions,
send order to your church.
Be love! O Guiding Spirit,
hear now our holy prayers.
We share one faith and love.

Refrain
All say as above.

Leader
Be love! O Mother Mary,
make all things come out well
and stay with us forever.
Be love! O John the Baptist,
unite us with the saints
and bring us to God's heart.
Be love! O Jesus Christ,
you save us from all harm
and lead us to salvation.

Refrain
All say as above.

Lead Us To The Water: Gathering

(Guitar/Vocal)

Tom Kendzia

Tom Kendzia and Gary Daigle

Lead Us To The Water: Dismissal
(Guitar/Vocal)

Tom Kendzia and Gary Daigle

LEAD US TO THE WATER: DISMISSAL (Guitar/Vocal), cont. (2)

As you prepare to provide adult formation in your parish, consider the following principles:

• *Formation needs to be systematic and comprehensive. Adults have a right to receive the faith in its purest form, and we leaders have a duty to present the faith as it was handed on to us by the church. At the same time, adults also have a right to be exposed to all the teachings of the church in a comprehensive manner. We should avoid a piecemeal approach that fragments the teachings of the church.*

• *Growing Faith can be used systematically by shaping various configurations of booklets into groups or modules. There are some suggestions for such use in Appendix II and a planning tool in Appendix I.*

Excerpts from

Our Hearts Were Burning Within Us

A Pastoral Plan for Adult Formation in the United States

3. The Church's pastoral ministry exists to sustain the work of the Gospel. One way it does this is by nourishing and strengthening lay men and women in their calling and identity as people of faith, as contributors to the life and work of the Church, and as disciples whose mission is to the world. To grow in discipleship throughout life, all believers need and are called to build vibrant parish and diocesan communities of faith and service.

4. Such communities cannot exist without a strong, complete, and systematic catechesis for all its members. By "complete and systematic" we mean a catechesis that nurtures a profound, lifelong conversion of the whole person and sets forth a comprehensive, contemporary synthesis of the faith, as presented in the *Catechism of the Catholic Church*. This catechesis will help adults to experience the transforming power of grace and to grasp the integrity and beauty of the truths of faith in their harmonious unity and interconnection—a true symphony of faith.

5. Adult faith formation, by which people consciously grow in the life of Christ through experience, reflection, prayer, and study, must be "the central task in [this] catechetical enterprise," becoming "the axis around which revolves the catechesis of childhood and adolescence as well as that of old age." This can be done specifically through developing in adults a better understanding of and participation in the full sacramental life of the Church.

6. To make this vision a reality, we, as the Catholic bishops of the United States, call the Church in our country to a renewed commitment to adult faith formation, positioning it at the heart of our catechetical vision and practice. We pledge to support adult faith formation without weakening our commitment to our other essential educational ministries. This pastoral plan guides the implementation of this pledge.

General Process for Using Growing Faith

In households, at the parish, in small communities, with youth and young adults, in nursing homes, with parents of school age children, and at parish meetings

1. Gather those who are going to take part in this session.

2. Make sure participants know one another. If there are newcomers or strangers, name tags are a great means of "breaking the ice."

3. As folks gather, even within the household or small group, play sacred music as a way of setting the stage and preparing the mind and heart.

4. Part of Christian hospitality is to provide food and refreshments. Members can help provide this on a rotating basis.

5. Once everyone is introduced and settled, begin with the opening prayer for *Growing Faith*: "Abide, O Spirit of Life" by Bill Huebsch. Or you can use the gathering song by Tom Kendzia, found on the PowerPoint CD-ROM accompanying this guide, which may be played either on a CD player or your computer.

6. The opening prayer and song are followed by a brief period of breaking open the word based on the Liturgy of the Word from the previous Sunday. Keep the sharing to a maximum of fifteen minutes. Notes on how to do this are included in other whole community catechesis resources, such as *Whole Community Catechesis in Plain English*, *Handbook for Success in Whole Community Catechesis*, and *Heritage of Faith*, all available from Twenty-Third Publications.

   You may also find a Question of the Week at Harcourt Religion's website: www.harcourtreligion.com. Click on whole community catechesis, then Question of the Week. Briefly, a simple, concrete question (Question of the Week) based on the theme of the Sunday readings is used by everyone in the parish community to encourage reflection, sharing, and positive action during the week.

7. Follow the notes in the Facilitator's Guide (which are reproducible) and work your way through the *Growing Faith* booklet for that evening. Take your time and do not rush this process. Let everyone have a chance to share, wonder about things aloud, and express his or her beliefs. If you don't finish the booklet, save the rest for next time.

8. Encourage participants to write notes in their booklets, to personalize them and own them. You may wish to provide a means by which folks can easily store and retrieve the booklets for ongoing use throughout their lives.

9. At the end of each gathering, make sure everyone knows when the next one will be held.

10. Close with the prayer on the last PowerPoint slide for each session, or with a spontaneous prayer. You can also use the closing song on the CD-ROM.

Preparation and Materials

Preparation

- Review the GF booklet for that gathering.
- Organize whatever food and other supplies will be needed.
- Assemble your volunteers for a one-hour rehearsal of the gathering.
- Make the room as welcoming as possible, using lighting, music, refreshments, and adequate signs to welcome people and help them find their place.
- This is an excellent opportunity for hospitality ministers within the parish to serve.
- Use name tags even if most participants know each other.
- As people arrive, have the first PowerPoint slide for that night on the screen, announcing the theme.

What you will need

- Food and beverages
- Name tags
- Computer and projector for PowerPoint presentation, and a screen large enough for the room; possibly a volunteer to help with technology
- Music to play as people arrive, and during breaks
- A Bible and copy of the *Catechism of the Catholic Church* for the facilitator
- If possible, personal Bibles for each participant
- Enough copies of the *Growing Faith* booklet for each participant
- Round tables, or rectangular tables organized so people can easily gather and hear one another
- The Scriptures enshrined within the room, along with a candle and other symbols of the faith
- A white, black, or paper board for writing notes as the group reports from small group activity to the large group
- A lectionary or guide for the Question of the Week

Suggestions for Use

Parish-wide, personal use

The invitation

- A large number of persons in every parish do not volunteer for parish leadership or ministry teams. They do not have children in school or religious education. They do not attend most parish functions, outside of Sunday Mass. However, they want to grow in their faith.
- *Growing Faith* provides the perfect tool for doing this. It is designed to be effective even when used privately.
- Invite anyone in the parish who wishes to grow in their faith to use *Growing Faith*, even if they do not wish to attend gatherings or meetings of any kind.
- You can hold two or three sign-up periods each year. You may want to schedule one for the early fall and another shortly after Christmas.
- For some people, private study of this kind is the best choice. Individuals should not be made to feel that group study is their only option.

The gathering

- Again, for some people, gathering may not be the right first step.
- Allow people to be part of parish life by studying at their own speed and at home.

The welcome

- Be clear in your announcements about *Growing Faith* that those who choose to use it individually, as well as those who choose to take part in a gathering, make the best choice for themselves personally. People should be trusted to know how and when they wish to enhance their journeys of faith. If we become purists about how we proceed, many people will never get the jump start that they need and want for their faith life.

Break open the word

- It is possible to break open the word alone. The Question of the Week should be sent home in the bulletin, posted on the parish website, and made available in any other possible way. Some people will look at the reading, consider the Question, and not share with anyone—and this is acceptable. We should affirm and support folks in their choice.

The process

- A person using *Growing Faith* privately does not need a session plan. *Growing Faith* is self-directing when used on an individual basis. This should allow anyone who wishes to grow in their faith to benefit from *Growing Faith*.

Follow-up

- Keep inviting folks to gather together for catechesis. Even though it is acceptable to study the faith on our own, individuals will benefit more by sharing at least part of this journey. Furthermore, as people study and grow spiritually, they will want to gather with others. New questions will arise in their minds. New desires will emerge in their hearts. Make room for everyone, and keep the door open to all.

Suggestions for Use

Families who have children in catechesis

The invitation

- This may be the most promising group with whom to use *Growing Faith*. Families are at that time of their lives where they want to pass their faith on to their children.
- This is why they enroll their children in religious education classes or in the parish school.
- Remember, however, that nearly half of families with children of elementary age do not participate fully in the life of the parish. The reasons for this vary from household to household.

What this group is experiencing in their faith

- Some families are active in the parish and excited about their faith. They may have made a retreat recently or encountered Christ on a deeper level.
- The faith of others, instead, has simply grown cold during their young adult years. They know how important their faith is, but they haven't been part of religious formation for many years. They feel unsure and, possibly, unwelcome.
- Still others are living in a marriage situation that the church does not condone or that they believe the church does not condone. Such situations may include

remarriage without annulment, living in a same-gender union, or living with a partner to whom they are not married. Others struggle as a single parent, in a household where more than one religious faith is present, in the aftermath of an abortion, in the aftermath of divorce even if no second marriage has taken place, or other conditions.

- Living in these settings does not mean they are separated from Christ, or that Christ has stopped loving them. When we invite them in the name of Christ to grow in their faith, we must bear all this in mind.
- All of these families attach some level of value to religion and religious upbringing. That's why they have enrolled their children in the school or catechetical process in the parish.

The gathering

- The best way to encourage these households to nurture their faith is to invite them to sponsor their own child for catechesis, even if only one parent is Catholic.
- You can organize assemblies or gatherings (see the *Handbook for Success in Whole Community Catechesis* for more on this). *Growing Faith* is designed for use in such public settings and creates an enjoyable way to explore the faith.
- Each booklet comes with a twelve slide PowerPoint presentation to aid in large group use. In addition a complete session plan is presented in part three of this guide.
- We must also be open to assisting families who wish to use *Growing Faith* at home.

The welcome

- For all the reasons mentioned above, let your welcome for these families be warm and genuine. Invite grandparents and other family members to be part of the process as well.
- If we wish to see people change their relationship with the church, the *Growing Faith* process is the best way to get them started.

Break open the word

- Use the Question of the Week for breaking open the word.
- Let the families lead this process themselves.
- Invite them to use Bibles of their own. Help them make the Bible their personal and treasured book. Teach them to write notes in the margins, to mark the texts they love most, and to be able to find the Sunday readings themselves.
- Make sure the Question of the Week is tailored for them.

The process

- If you are gathering for intergenerational assemblies, the session plans in part three of this guide for each *Growing Faith* booklet will work perfectly.

- If you have parents gathering separately from their children during regular catechesis sessions, again those session plans will serve you well.
- The best way for families to learn is to study what their children are studying. *Growing Faith* is designed for this. When the children are studying creation and revelation, for example, their families should be too.
- In some settings, this will mean one *Growing Faith* booklet for each lesson in the children's book. For others, it may mean following one of the *Growing Faith* configurations outlined in the appendices of this guide.

Afterward

- We know that if a child learns his or her religion lesson perfectly in the school or parish religious education class, but goes home to a place where the faith is not cherished or understood, that child's faith will probably not grow to maturity.
- For this reason, bringing families into the learning circle as their child grows is not optional; it is essential.
- Urge families to take home the *Growing Faith* booklets, and to read and reflect on them. You may wish to give them copies of the index at the back of this guide for their own use. Along with their Bible, *Growing Faith* should occupy a central place in their homes.

Suggestions for Use

Catechumens and candidates in the RCIA process

The invitation

- The truths of the Catholic faith are rooted in the deepest recesses of what it means to be authentically human. When you invite people to explore these truths using *Growing Faith*, you offer them a glimpse into the holy and into the human heart. This is a powerful experience.
- Keep offering. Make your welcome strong and far-reaching. Continue to assure people that they will find here the seeds of eternity, the bread of life which satisfies the hunger in their hearts.

- The normal process of inviting people to the catechumenate involves use of the local newspapers, parish bulletins, outreach to family members, and other means.
- Conduct your inquiry sessions in the RCIA as you normally would.

The gathering

- Once the inquiry period comes to an end and the process of learning about the Catholic faith begins, gather the catechumens for this purpose.
- Most of the time, these gatherings are rather small, perhaps ten or twenty in number. This is a perfect setting for using *Growing Faith*.
- Make sure the room you use is welcoming and that each person who comes through the door feels welcome. Use name tags often, wearing one yourself if you're the leader. Have refreshments available as part of your hospitality, or perhaps even a simple meal.
- Use a room that contains symbols of our faith such as a crucifix, sacred art, an enshrined copy of our Sacred Scriptures, and so forth. The ambience and symbols form part of the teaching environment.

The welcome

- Let people take part as often as they can in this process, and stay as long as they want. No one can be forced to love the faith, or to join the church. Let each one's individual journey of faith unfold. But make sure you welcome everyone, regardless of their situation in life.

Break open the word

- In the catechumenate especially, this activity is ongoing and important because we know that, by sharing our faith with each other, we ourselves experience a transformation of our hearts, which is conversion to Christ.

The process

- Follow the session plans presented in part three of this guide, allowing plenty of time for sharing. The PowerPoint presentation may be awkward to use if the group is too small. The session plans are written to work with or without the PowerPoint presentation.
- The best course of study for persons in this group is to begin with *Growing Faith* booklet one and continue to the end. This will provide a systematic and comprehensive presentation of the Catholic faith.
- Take your time in presenting and processing the material in *Growing Faith*. It is a rich resource with many opportunities for reflection and exploration.

Afterward

- Many times, folks exploring their faith have personal issues to talk through, or events from their past lives which they may want to resolve. Provide the means for this by offering contact through you. Be prepared to make the connections with the pastor, pastoral care in the parish, or outside counseling services. Be available to speak with them about what's on their minds as their journey of faith unfolds.

- Urge participants to collect these booklets and reread them often as they grow in their faith. Feel free to provide participants with a photocopy of the index provided in the appendices of this guide.

Suggestions for Use

Pastoral councils, pastoral ministers, and other leaders

The invitation

- The US bishops' pastoral letter on adult faith formation, *Our Hearts Were Burning Within Us*, suggests that every time a parish meeting is held an opportunity exists for catechesis.

- Invite those who come forward as leaders in your parish to spend a little extra time at each of their meetings to learn more about their faith.

- Leaders would include but not be limited to the pastoral council, pastoral ministers, all committees and sub-committees, the sodalities and fraternal groups of the parish such as the Knights of Columbus and the Catholic Daughters, and any other group that meets regularly.

The rationale

- Parish leaders and ministry team members, more than anyone else in the parish, must be well-versed in their faith. However, most adults in the church today are working from an elementary level catechesis.

- Therefore, spending twenty extra minutes at each meeting to study Catholic teaching in more depth is one way to enhance their role as baptized members of the church, sharing in the priestly, prophetic, and royal work of Christ. Their calling as leaders involves helping the faithful grow in holiness, teaching others about our faith, and governing the local church.

- Studying the faith, sharing faith, and growing in faith also draw the group members closer to one another, thus creating real community.

The gathering

- Using *Growing Faith* during your parish meetings is easy. Simply gather in the same room around the same table you will use for the meeting.

Break open the word

- People who volunteer to serve in leadership groups in the parish are giving precious time to the parish community. They want to attend the meetings, get the work done, and return home. Most lay volunteers also hold full-time jobs inside or outside the home.

- Yet, unless we break open the word together, we risk losing our central purpose, which is to know Christ and to help others know Christ, too. So don't be tempted to skip this step in the interest of saving time.

- Instead, let it be known from the outset that being part of parish leadership and ministry also involves sharing faith and studying church teachings. It means growing in our relationship with Christ.

The process

- The notes in the session plans presented in part three of this guide are written to work in settings such as these. The three-part process allows everyone to take part: (1) read and reflect for a moment, (2) share faith with others, and (3) find ways to take home what they've learned or apply it in their meeting.

- For these groups, it might be best if you plan to cover fewer booklets in one year, rather than the entire series. In your long-term plan you can make sure that, over a two or three year period, you provide a systematic and comprehensive presentation of the faith for everyone.

Afterward

- Make sure that everyone receives their own copies of the *Growing Faith* booklet and make them their own. Urge them to write notes in them, to write down questions as they arise, and to note what others share.

Suggestions for Use

Youth groups, faith formation for high school students, and confirmation programs

Organizing for youth groups

- Work in three seasons each year, roughly coordinated with the local high school calendar:

    Fall

    Winter

    Spring

- Select a GF course for each season. GF is designed to be used with young people over a two-year period for three seasons of gatherings per year, with eight gatherings per season. Confirmation students will thus receive a systematic and comprehensive course of the Catholic faith before they celebrate the sacrament.
- Combine youth ministry and high school faith formation events on a fifty-fifty basis.

One month before each season starts

- Begin advertising in the parish bulletin and websites, and get the word out person to person among the youth.
- Schedule events at a minimum of every two weeks to keep the energy flowing.
- Prepare volunteers among the older youth to help arrange the meeting space.
- Make sure you have enough copies of the GF booklets needed for that season.
- Invite the pastor or other appropriate pastoral staff to be present.

The welcome

- Make your welcome warm and genuine. Remember, at least half of the youth members of your parish are living in homes where there is minimal participation in the Sunday assembly.

Break open the word

- Use the Question of the Week for breaking open the word.
- Let the young people lead this process themselves.

- Invite them to use Bibles of their own. Help them make the Bible their personal and treasured book. Teach them to write notes in the margins, to mark the texts they love most, and to be able to find the Sunday readings themselves.
- Make sure the Question of the Week is tailored for youth members. You might want to call this activity "checking in" rather than "faith sharing" as you begin. Above all, let them talk.

The process

- Each *Growing Faith* booklet is designed to be used in three short sections, all within a single gathering. Use the step-by-step session plan for each booklet to lead this process. These session plans are presented in part three of this guide.
- Allow plenty of time for discussion and conversation among the young people.
- Be creative about adding various age appropriate exercises as you plan.
- At the end, announce other youth ministry activities and be sure to leave plenty of time for informal socializing.

Afterward

- Keep an open door for young people, even if they question their faith.
- Invite them to speak with you personally and privately if needed, or help them connect with the pastor, pastoral staff, or local counseling services.
- Make sure they always know when the next gathering will be. Keep the ball rolling. Excitement builds when the time between gatherings is short.
- Encourage teens to invite their friends. Use the web or e-mail to stay in touch; allow them to contact you or others when they need or want to.
- Urge them to collect the *Growing Faith* booklets and reread them often.

Suggestions for Use

Young adults and campus ministry

Organizing

- Assign someone in the parish, paid staff or volunteer, to get to know the young adults and to stay in touch with them.

- If you have a junior college, vocational training school, college, or other school of higher learning in your parish, and it does not have an organized campus ministry program, treat your approach to the students there as campus ministry.

Some characteristics of this group

- There are few common denominators after high school. Some adults marry quickly and start families. Others remain single for many years. Some do not pursue any further education after high school, or perhaps did not complete high school itself. Others go on to higher education. Some are very connected to the parish. Others are very disconnected.
- Some young adults mistrust institutions, including the church. They believe institutions serve mainly those in authority.
- Almost everyone in this group has grown up in an age of pluralism. Diversity is everywhere today, even in the smallest towns. Because of this people see most situations and religious claims as one among many. This means that, rather than holding religious belief as absolute truth, they consider it simply a viewpoint. They see value, richness, and even deep validity in other religious beliefs. Figurative and mythical religious language and categories often play poorly among individuals in this group. Finally, young adults seek spirituality. They have a strong sense of an inner life that many want to develop but without a specific religious affiliation.

The invitation

- If we invite young people to join a parish and sign up for an education program, we will miss the mark.
- But if we offer them help on their spiritual journey and share with them the deep insights of the Catholic faith, we will persuade with the power of our faith and witness rather than by insistence and demands.

The gathering

- The gatherings for young adults may be done through electronic means at first. Develop your parish website to meet their needs, and use e-mail as much as possible to stay in touch with them. If your youth faith formation process is effective, that will also help nourish formation during young adulthood. Some means might include online chat rooms, booklet reading clubs, and similar gatherings, which can lead to taking part in assemblies.

The welcome

- Welcome the folks in this age group to take part as often as they can, and to stay as long as they want. Keep it simple. Speaking of lifelong commitments to the church or even to Christ might be too much to begin with. Instead, offer them a chance to connect with each other, a chance to talk about how faith fits into their lives.

Break open the word

- Use the Question of the Week for breaking open the word.
- Let the young adults lead this process themselves.
- Invite them to use Bibles of their own. Help them make the Bible their personal and treasured book. Teach them to write notes in the margins, to mark the texts they love most, and to be able to find the Sunday readings themselves.
- Make sure the Question of the Week is tailored for young adults.

The process

- Follow the session plans for each booklet in part three of this guide, but don't be a slave to them. Allow the conversation to flow naturally.
- One way to honor every question or challenge while at the same time moving ahead so the entire text can be presented, is to keep a running list of issues and questions on a paper chart. This allows you to table certain issues until later in the *Growing Faith* process. Each booklet covers a limited number of topics.

Afterward

- Urge the young adults of the parish to keep these *Growing Faith* booklets as their own. Encourage them to return to the text between sessions, to read and reflect again on these teachings.
- Stay in touch as often as you can between gatherings, using whatever means you have: phone, e-mail, websites, personal visits.
- Encourage them to invite their friends to the next gathering.

Suggestions for Use

Middle-aged and senior adults

Invitation

- This is often a time of life when:
  - Folks have a little more time to study and read because the busy years of child raising or professional work may be winding down or ended.
  - There is a greater curiosity about religion and faith.

– Some people have more disposable income to afford study materials.

– Many of these folks are single again, or have always remained single.

– In today's church, many persons in these groups have not had formal religious formation for several years.

– Inviting them personally to either join with others or work alone to grow in their faith is beneficial for them and for the faith community.

– These people are often overlooked precisely because they no longer have children in parish programs.

The gathering

• These adults may use *Growing Faith* in any of the ways discussed in this guide:

– In small Christian communities

– Within households of faith

– With family members, friends, or neighbors in the intergenerational assemblies being held within the parish (if they are open to all parish members)

– In their own homes

– As volunteers in parish leadership groups or ministry teams.

The welcome

• These groups are a rich resource for the life of the parish community. Welcome them warmly to study and grow in their faith.

• Welcome their non-Catholic spouses with them. Many of them have been sharing home life for decades. Why not invite couples to share their faith life as well?

Break open the word

• Use the Question of the Week for breaking open the word.

• Let the participants lead this process themselves.

• Invite them to use Bibles of their own. Help them make the Bible their personal and treasured book.

• Make sure the Question of the Week is tailored for them.

The process

• Use the session plans booklet presented in part three of this guide to gather and study each booklet of *Growing Faith*.

• The best course of study would be to begin with *Growing Faith* booklet number one and proceed to the end. But in some settings, it may work better to follow one of the other configurations of booklets outlined in the appendices to this guide.

Suggestions for Use

Small Christian communities in your parish

The invitation

- It's an excellent practice to schedule regular sign-up periods for people interested in taking part in small Christian communities.
- Such communities usually gather in members' homes on a rotating basis, but some also gather at the parish. The gathering is normally two to three hours long, includes refreshments of some kind, and follows a course of conversation and study.
- The best way to help non-participants understand the benefits of small community life is through witness. Brief post-communion presentations will reach the largest audience.

The welcome

- Small communities can make everyone feel welcome in parish life. If possible, child care can be provided to assist single parents on limited incomes to take part.

Break open the word

- Use the Question of the Week for breaking open the word.
- Let the participants lead this process themselves.
- Invite them to use Bibles of their own. Help them make the Bible their personal and treasured book.
- Make sure the Question of the Week is tailored for them.

The process

- The session plans presented in part three of this guide can easily be adapted for small community use.
- The best choice for small communities is to begin with *Growing Faith* booklet one and complete them all to the end. This will provide a systematic and comprehensive view of the Catholic faith.
- Don't rush the process. Each booklet is filled with teachings and ideas. Take time to move through the explorations and reflections together. The group may need two or three meetings to fully process a single booklet.

Afterward

- Encourage members to keep their booklets and reread them again and again. Faith is a lifelong journey, and growing in our faith takes place gradually. By returning to various parts of the booklets when the right moment arises in one's journey, our faith is nourished and fed.

Suggestions for Use

Intergenerational catechetical gatherings

Gathering the participants

These gatherings may be organized according to one of the following plans:

- *Intergenerational model*
  Children and adults are in the same room.
  The gathering is open to everyone in the parish.
  Special focus is on inviting parents with children in the process.
  Adults, youth, and young adults use *Growing Faith* in conjunction with the children's curriculum.
- *Combination model*
  Start with everyone in the same room. Use *Growing Faith* to introduce the theme and topics for the evening to the whole group.
  Send children to age-based gatherings with catechists.
  Send adults to their own gathering, using *Growing Faith* as the resource.
  Close with shared prayer and refreshments.
- *All-at-one-time model*
  Gather the children in traditional religious education classrooms for the catechetical process.
  Gather adults in a separate space to use *Growing Faith*. Both adults and children study the same themes.
  Close with shared prayer and refreshments.

The invitation

- All of the models suggested for use can welcome people from the whole community, whether or not they have children enrolled in the catechesis process.

- Be sure to include teenagers and young adults in the invitation. Also include students at nearby universities, colleges, vocational training schools, and others if there is no campus ministry available to them.

One month before each season starts

- Begin advertising in the bulletin and on websites. Get the word out person to person among the members of the parish. Invite young people, the confirmation groups, or any group you wish to reach with catechesis.
- Schedule these gatherings regularly to keep the energy flowing and to help people include them in their personal schedules.
- Prepare volunteers to help arrange the meeting space.
- Make sure you have enough copies of the GF booklets needed for that season.
- Invite the pastor or other appropriate pastoral staff members to be present.

One week before each gathering

- Review the GF booklet for that gathering.
- Organize whatever food and other supplies will be needed.
- Assemble your volunteers for a one-hour rehearsal of the gathering.

The Assembly Format

The welcome (three minutes)

- Welcome the non-Catholic spouses or any guests who attend.
- Welcome all newcomers without making them feel uncomfortable.
- Make your welcome warm and genuine.
- If possible, the welcome can come from several people: pastor, process leader, pastoral council leaders, or others.

The leaders (two minutes)

- Ask each table group to choose someone to serve as leader.
- No special training is needed. This person's role is to keep the process moving during the discussion, to take notes, and to speak on behalf of the table group to the large group.

The song and breaking open the word (fifteen minutes)

- Ask the group to focus and observe a moment of silence before beginning. Use the *Growing Faith* prayer, "Abide, O Spirit of Life," by Bill Huebsch. You will also find a gathering song on the PowerPoint CD-ROM that can be played on either a CD player or your computer.

- Follow that opening with 15 minutes of faith sharing based on the Question of the Week. Briefly, a simple, concrete question (Question of the Week) based on the theme of the Sunday readings is used by everyone in the parish community to encourage reflection, sharing, and positive action during the week. More details about how to do this are found in other whole community catechesis resources.

The process

Growing Faith, part one (forty minutes)

- Follow the notes in the session plans presented in part three of this guide for the booklet you are using during that meeting.
- Use the PowerPoint slides as noted.

Break (fifteen minutes)

Growing Faith, part two (forty minutes)

- Resume where you left off before the break.

Closing (five minutes)

- Invite people to take the *Growing Faith* booklets home and save them.
- Urge them to bring along other family members or friends to the next gathering.
- Close with the simple prayer on the last PowerPoint slide (see below), or use the prayer of Blessed John XXIII on page 5 of this guide.

Leader	Let us pray…
All	Oh, God, we know that you are with us and that you know everything we say and do. By the light of your Holy Spirit, may we be diligent in our journey of faith and loving toward others. We ask this through Christ our Lord. Amen.
Leader	Go in peace!

Suggestions for Use

Households of faith within your parish

The invitation

- Nothing is more important to the church than developing our households as "domestic churches."

- An excellent way to do so is to offer them a weekly purpose for gathering, such as *Growing Faith*.
- *Growing Faith* booklets are user-friendly and self-directing. Households do not need to purchase copies of this facilitator's guide.
- Offer households the opportunity to sign up for this process in the autumn and again shortly after the Christmas holidays.

The gathering

- Many households are not accustomed to gathering for faith sharing and study. As a parish leader, you can help them by affirming their efforts and providing useful materials.
- Encourage your households to gather on Sunday evenings if possible, for about two hours. Including a household meal in the process is an excellent practice.
- Single folks may be invited to join friends or acquaintances. The parish may provide a means for single people living alone to meet others for the purpose of household based gatherings.
- Invite the children of the home to join right in! Even if they're a bit noisy or distracted, by joining you in the household sharing, they learn how important religion is in our lives.

Break open the word

- Each household gathering should begin with fifteen minutes of breaking open the word, using the resources available on the whole community catechesis website, from your local parish, or in a variety of printed resources.

The process

- The best way to proceed, of course, is to start with *Growing Faith* booklet one and proceed to the end, thereby obtaining a systematic and comprehensive presentation of the Catholic faith and how to live it in daily life.
- Some households may prefer to choose from among the *Growing Faith* configurations of booklets outlined in the appendices of this guide.
- The booklets are self-directing.

Afterward

- Encourage families to have and maintain a full collection of *Growing Faith* booklets of their own. Provide copies of the index found at the back of this guide. It will help them find answers to questions about the faith.

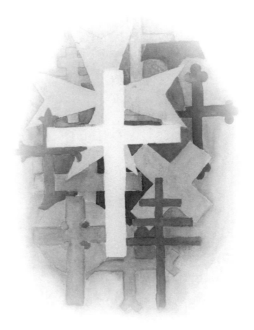

Session Plans

for each of the forty-eight booklets

Session Plan for Reflection Booklet **1**

What Does Your Heart Desire?

Content summary

The inborn hunger for God (based on articles 26–49 in the *Catechism of the Catholic Church*)

- We are religious beings by nature.
- We are made to live in communion with God.
- Being with God is the only way to find happiness.
- When we listen to the message of creation and to the voice of conscience, we can reason with certainty about the existence of God.

Preparation

- Read through the booklet once, reflectively. Reread it and make your own notes.
- Read through the session plan and become comfortable with the format.
- For more background, read articles 26–49 of the *Catechism*. Mark and look up any unfamiliar words.
- Decide if and when you will do the exercise found after the material for pages six and seven. Have the materials needed.
- See pages 12–13 in this guide for other steps for preparation and materials needed.

Opening

- After introductions, if the number of participants is ten or more, ask them to form small groups. If the assembly is a large one, have each group choose a spokesperson.
- Have PowerPoint slide 1 (the cover illustration) on the screen as you begin.
- Open with the prayer found on page 4 in the introductory section of this guide. You may make copies for the participants. Or use the gathering song on the CD.
- Use the Question of the Week approach to break open the word of God from the Sunday liturgy (see 6 on page 12). Then continue with the *Growing Faith* booklet.

Pages two and three

Read and reflect

- Make sure everyone has a copy of the booklet.
- Ask the participants to read pages two and three of the booklet quietly. Tell them they will have a few minutes to do so (about five minutes).
- Invite them to mark the text when they read something that strikes them.

Share it with others

- Read the reflection on slide 2 and/or the reflection(s) provided in the booklet. Ask participants to discuss these questions in their small groups as a means of applying what they have learned in the text. Encourage them to take notes in their booklets. Give them several minutes to do all this. You may wish to play quiet music in the background during this time.
- If the assembly is large, ask the spokesperson of each small group to share a summary of the group's discussion with the larger group. Write on the board a short version or outline of all the responses.
- Use the PowerPoint slide 3 to provide the group with a visual of a Scripture passage. Open your Bibles to Psalms 42:1, and select a few verses to read aloud. How does this Scripture passage relate to what you have just read and discussed?
- Pause for a few moments of silence, then go to the illustration on slide 4, which is also found in the booklet. Ask the participants to look at the illustration. On the back cover you will find a reference for this illustration, from Scripture or the *Catechism*, that may assist you. Explain that we humans have the ability to look within ourselves and find a spiritual core. Such searching requires that we spend time alone, or with a trusted friend or two. The woman carrying the basket represents each of us, made in God's image and searching for God.
- Invite feedback about this illustration and its commentary (about five minutes).

Break

Pages four and five

The illustration

- Show the illustration on slide 5, which is the same as the one on pages four and five in the booklet. Invite the participants to look at the illustration. Ask questions such as: Can you relate to this image of the young man walking along the beach? How? Think of some moments when you were especially aware of God's presence.

- Refer to the quote on the back cover. "The desire for God is written in [our hearts] because [we are] created by God and for God." Although other desires may get in the way, ultimately we cannot be happy unless we continually seek and serve God in our lives in response to God's love. The universe God created is so tremendous, yet God never forgets us! As St. Augustine observes, the beauty of the earth itself is a profession of faith.
- Invite other feedback about this illustration and its commentary (about five minutes).

Read and reflect

- Ask participants to read pages four and five. Follow the same process for reading and reflection that you used for the first pages.

Share it with others

- Read the reflection on slide 6 and/or the reflection(s) provided in the booklet. Use the same format for group discussion and sharing as you did for the previous pages.
- Use PowerPoint slide 7 to provide the group with a visual of a Scripture passage. Open your Bibles to Wisdom 13:5, and select a few verses to read aloud. How does this Scripture passage relate to what you have just read and discussed?
- Pause for a few moments of silence.

Pages six and seven

Personal experience

- Ask everyone to look at the first heading on page six, "We see ourselves." Invite them to reflect on these questions: What do I see when I look in the mirror? Just a face? Just a body? How often do I remember that I am so much more than that?
- Hand out sheets of blank paper and pencils and ask them to draw a simple but real picture of themselves, or symbols representing themselves.

Read and reflect

- Again, follow the same process for reading and reflection on pages six and seven. Share it with others.
- Read the reflection on slide 8 and/or the reflection(s) provided in the booklet. Use the same format for group discussion and sharing.
- Use PowerPoint slide 9 to provide the group with a visual of a Scripture passage. Open your Bibles to 1 John 1:5, and select a few verses to read aloud. How does this Scripture passage relate to what you have just read and discussed?

- Pause for a few moments of silence, then go to the illustration on slide 10, which is the same as the one on pages six and seven. Ask the participants to look at the illustration. Refer to the corresponding quote on the back cover. The parish to which we belong is our part of the larger Catholic community worldwide. No matter how large or small a parish family is, we are all united in the church. We seek God and learn more about God and ourselves through our parish community.

Exercise

- If time permits, at some point invite participants to do the exercise on page three: creating their own life chart. This exercise is an excellent tool for helping them reflect on their journey with God. Suggest that after they complete it—either during the gathering or at home—they might want to share it with someone close to them, such as a family member, a friend, and so on.

Take it home

- Before the end of the evening, ask the small groups to talk once more about how they plan to take home and live what they have learned. Refer to the reflections, and suggest they use them to help apply the core message of this booklet. Invite them to make concrete and realistic plans. Allow a few minutes for this discussion.

Conclusion

- Go to slide 11 and announce the time and place of the next gathering.
- Go to slide 12 and invite everyone to pray the closing prayer aloud. (You can make copies of the prayer, found on page 29 of this guide, or use the prayer of Blessed John XXIII on page 5.) You can, instead, invite the group to offer spontaneous prayer. You may also close the evening with the dismissal song on the CD.

Session Plan for Reflection Booklet **2**

Where Do You Meet God?

Content summary

God reveals a loving plan (based on articles 50–73 in the *Catechism of the Catholic Church*)

- Out of love, God has revealed and given himself to us.
- God reveals the divine to us by gradually communicating God's own mystery in deeds and in words.
- God has communicated himself to us from the beginning of the human race.
- God has revealed himself fully through Jesus Christ, in whom God has established an eternal covenant.

Preparation

- Read through the booklet once, reflectively. Reread it and make your own notes.
- Read through the session plan and become comfortable with the format.
- For more background, read articles 50–73 of the *Catechism*. Mark and look up any unfamiliar words.
- Decide if and when you will do the exercise found after the material for pages six and seven. Have the materials needed.
- See pages 12–13 in this guide for other steps for preparation and materials needed.

Opening

- After introductions, if the number of participants is ten or more, ask them to form small groups. If the assembly is a large one, have each group choose a spokesperson.
- Have PowerPoint slide 1 (the cover illustration) on the screen as you begin.
- Open with the prayer found on page 4 in the introductory section of this guide. You may make copies for the participants. Or use the gathering song on the CD.
- Use the Question of the Week approach to break open the word of God from the Sunday liturgy (see 6 on page 12). Then continue with the *Growing Faith* booklet.

Pages two and three

Read and reflect

- Make sure everyone has a copy of the booklet.
- Ask the participants to read pages two and three of the booklet quietly. Tell them they will have a few minutes to do so (about five minutes).
- Invite them to mark the text when they read something that strikes them.

Share it with others

- Read the reflection on slide 2 and/or the reflection(s) provided in the booklet. Ask participants to discuss these questions in their small groups as a means of applying what they have learned in the text. Encourage them to take notes in their booklets. Give them several minutes to do all this. You may wish to play quiet music in the background during this time.
- If the assembly is large, ask the spokesperson of each small group to share a summary of the group's discussion with the larger group. Write on the board a short version or outline of all the responses.
- Use the PowerPoint slide 3 to provide the group with a visual of a Scripture passage. Open your Bibles to Ephesians 1:11, and select a few verses to read aloud. How does this Scripture passage relate to what you have just read and discussed?
- Pause for a few moments of silence, then go to the illustration on slide 4, which is also found in the booklet. Ask the participants to look at the illustration. On the back cover you will find a reference for this illustration, from Scripture or the *Catechism*, that may assist you. God has often spoken through persons we would least expect: the poor, the disenfranchised, the rejected. Through whom is God speaking today?
- Invite feedback and general conversation on this illustration and its commentary (about five minutes).

Break

Pages four and five

The illustration

- Show the illustration on slide 5, which is the same as the one in the booklet. Invite the participants to look at the illustration. Ask questions such as: What is a tree? What does a tree mean to you? How does creation help you believe more deeply in God?

- Refer to the quote on the back cover. "God provides [us] with constant evidence of himself." God communicates himself to us through creation. God has also communicated himself to us through his chosen ones, through a people and a covenant. Has God made a covenant with you? How and when?
- Invite feedback on this illustration and its commentary (about 5 minutes).

Read and reflect

- Ask participants to read pages four and five. Follow the same process for reading and reflection that you used for the first pages.

Share it with others

- Read the reflection on slide 6 and/or the reflection(s) provided in the booklet. Use the same format for group discussion and sharing as you did for the previous pages.
- Use PowerPoint slide 7 to provide the group with a visual of a Scripture passage. Open your Bibles to Jeremiah 31:31, and select a few verses to read aloud. How does this Scripture passage relate to what you have just read and discussed?
- Pause for a few moments of silence.

Pages six and seven

Personal experience

- Ask everyone to look at the first heading on page six, "God's Word." Invite them to reflect on these questions: What and how many words do I hear during the day? Where do I hear God's word? Do I look for God's word only in the Scriptures or during the Mass?
- Keep a journal of the times you hear God's words during the day, and from whom.

Read and reflect

- Again, follow the same process for reading and reflection on pages six and seven.

Share it with others

- Read the reflection on slide 8 and/or the reflection(s) provided in the booklet. Use the same format for group discussion and sharing.
- Use PowerPoint slide 9 to provide the group with a visual of a Scripture passage. Open your Bibles to John 14:16, and select a few verses to read aloud. How does this Scripture passage relate to what you have just read and discussed?

- Pause for a few moments of silence, then go to the illustration on slide 10, which is the same as the one on these pages. Ask the participants to look at the illustration. Refer to the quote on the back cover. Sharing meals is the primary way we encounter and share thoughts with each other, not only on important feast days, but also on an everyday basis. Meals are the backbone of life. Jesus spoke some of his most important words at meals. What meals did Jesus share with his followers? What other "meal" do Catholics share? What part does God's word play at that meal?

Exercise

- The timeline described in the Exercise on page four could be done as a group project, if time permits. Use a large piece of white butcher paper or several sheets of construction paper, and pencils or markers. Each person in the group could do a different section of the timeline. If possible, attach or draw pictures appropriate for the different persons and time periods.
- If time doesn't permit you to do this during the session, suggest that the participants might enjoy completing this exercise as a family project.

Take it home

- Before the end of the evening, ask the small groups to talk once more about how they plan to take home and live what they have learned. Refer to the reflections, and suggest they use them to help apply the core message of this booklet. Invite them to make concrete and realistic plans. Allow a few minutes for this discussion.

Conclusion

- Go to slide 11 and announce the time and place of the next gathering.
- Go to slide 12 and invite everyone to pray the closing prayer aloud. (You can make copies of the prayer, found on page 29 of this guide, or use the prayer of Blessed John XXIII on page 5.) You can, instead, invite the group to offer spontaneous prayer. You may also close the evening with the dismissal song on the CD.

Session Plan for Reflection Booklet **3**

Why Do We Need the Church?

Content summary

The Church passes on divine revelation (based on articles 74–100 in the *Catechism of the Catholic Church*)

- What Christ entrusted to the apostles, they in turn handed on to all generations through their preaching and writing, under the inspiration of the Holy Spirit.
- Sacred Tradition and Sacred Scripture form a single sacred statement of the word of God.
- The pilgrim church contemplates God, the source of all her riches.
- The church, in her doctrine, life, and worship, passes on to all of us everything she believes.

Preparation

- Read through the booklet once, reflectively. Reread it and make your own notes.
- Read through the session plan and become comfortable with the format.
- For more background, read articles 74–100 of the *Catechism*. Mark and look up any unfamiliar words.
- Decide if and when you will do the exercise found after the material for pages six and seven. Have the materials needed.
- See pages 12–13 in this guide for other steps for preparation and materials needed.

Opening

- After introductions, if the number of participants is ten or more, ask them to form small groups. If the assembly is a large one, have each group choose a spokesperson.
- Have PowerPoint slide 1 (the cover illustration) on the screen as you begin.
- Open with the prayer found on page 4 in the introductory section of this guide. You may make copies for the participants. Or use the gathering song on the CD.
- Use the Question of the Week approach to break open the word of God from the Sunday liturgy (see 6 on page 12). Then continue with the *Growing Faith* booklet.

Pages two and three

Read and reflect

- Make sure everyone has a copy of the booklet.
- Ask the participants to read pages two and three of the booklet quietly. Tell them they will have a few minutes to do so (about five minutes).
- Invite them to mark the text when they read something that strikes them.

Share it with others

- Read the reflection on slide 2 and/or the reflection(s) provided in the booklet. Ask participants to discuss these questions in their small groups as a means of applying what they have learned in the text. Encourage them to take notes in their booklets. Give them several minutes to do all this. You may wish to play quiet music in the background during this time.
- If the assembly is large, ask the spokesperson of each small group to share a summary of the group's discussion with the larger group. Write on the board a short version or outline of all the responses.
- Use the PowerPoint slide 3 to provide the group with a visual of a Scripture passage. Open your Bibles to John 1:1, and select a few verses to read aloud. How does this Scripture passage relate to what you have just read and discussed?
- Pause for a few moments of silence, then go to the illustration on slide 4, which is also found in the booklet. Ask the participants to look at the illustration. On the back cover you will find a reference for this illustration, from Scripture or the *Catechism*, that may assist you. For us Christians, God speaks through the Scriptures. Each time we hear the word and "break it open," we are touched by the Holy Spirit.
- Invite feedback and general conversation about this illustration and its commentary (about five minutes).

Break

Pages four and five

The illustration

- Show the illustration on slide 5, which is the same as the one in the booklet. Invite the participants to look at the illustration. Ask questions such as: Can you relate to this image? How much time do you spend each week studying the Bible? Do you use a commentary or Scripture study guide?

- Refer to the quote on the back cover. "Blessed are those who hear the word of God." By studying the Scriptures we come to an ever deeper love of God and understanding of what God wants for our lives. We live then by the light of faith.
- Invite feedback on this illustration and its commentary (about 5 minutes).

Read and reflect

- Ask participants to read pages four and five. Follow the same process for reading and reflection that you used for the first pages.

Share it with others

- Read the reflection on slide 6 and/or the reflection(s) provided in the booklet. Use the same format for group discussion and sharing as you did for the previous pages.
- Use PowerPoint slide 7 to provide the group with a visual of a Scripture passage. Open your Bibles to Matthew 28:20, and select a few verses to read aloud. How does this Scripture passage relate to what you have just read and discussed?
- Pause for a few moments of silence.

Pages six and seven

Personal experience

- Ask everyone to look at the first heading on page six, "The deposit of faith." Invite them to reflect on questions such as: What does the word "deposit" mean to me? How valuable are the things I deposit? What do I think is the relationship between "deposit" and "faith"?

Read and reflect

- Again, follow the same process for reading and reflection on pages six and seven.

Share it with others

- Read the reflection on slide 8 and/or the reflection(s) provided in the booklet. Use the same format for group discussion and sharing.
- Use PowerPoint slide 9 to provide the group with a visual of a Scripture passage. Open your Bibles to John 16:13, and select a few verses to read aloud. How does this Scripture passage relate to what you have just read and discussed?

- Pause for a few moments of silence, then go to the illustration on slide 10, which is the same as the one on these pages. Ask the participants to look at the illustration. Refer to the quote on the back cover. Pope John XXIII had a profound understanding of his great call to love all men and women as Christ would love them. When we are truly of Christ, no one is turned away and everyone is welcome. Judgment takes a "back burner."

Exercise

- At some point have each group make a list of the traditions they and their families practice. How did these develop? How important are these traditions in preserving their faith and culture? If time does not allow you to do this exercise during the session, suggest that the members do it with their families.

Take it home

- Before the end of the evening, ask the small groups to talk once more about how they plan to take home and live what they have learned. Refer to the reflections, and suggest they use them to help apply the core message of this booklet. Invite them to make concrete and realistic plans. Allow a few minutes for this discussion.

Conclusion

- Go to slide 11 and announce the time and place of the next gathering.
- Go to slide 12 and invite everyone to pray the closing prayer aloud. (You can make copies of the prayer, found on page 29 of this guide, or use the prayer of Blessed John XXIII on page 5.) You can, instead, invite the group to offer spontaneous prayer. You may also close the evening with the dismissal song on the CD.

Session Plan for Reflection Booklet 4

How Does God Speak to Us?

Content summary

Scripture is the word of God (based on articles 101–141 in the *Catechism of the Catholic Church*)

- God is the author of sacred Scripture because God inspired its human authors.
- Interpretation of Scripture must be attentive above all to what God wants to reveal through the writings of the sacred authors.
- The Church accepts and venerates as inspired the 46 books of the Old Testament and the 27 books of the New Testament.
- The four gospels occupy a central place because Christ Jesus is their center.

Preparation

- Read through the booklet once, reflectively. Reread it and make your own notes.
- Read through the session plan and become comfortable with the format.
- For more background, read articles 101–141 of the *Catechism*. Mark and look up any unfamiliar words.
- Decide if and when you will do the exercise found after the material for pages six and seven. Have the materials needed.
- See pages 12–13 in this guide for other steps for preparation and materials needed.

Opening

- After introductions, if the number of participants is ten or more, ask them to form small groups. If the assembly is a large one, have each group choose a spokesperson.
- Have PowerPoint slide 1 (the cover illustration) on the screen as you begin.
- Open with the prayer found on page 4 in the introductory section of this guide. You may make copies for the participants. Or use the gathering song on the CD.
- Use the Question of the Week approach to break open the word of God from the Sunday liturgy (see 6 on page 12). Then continue with the *Growing Faith* booklet.

Pages two and three

Read and reflect

- Make sure everyone has a copy of the booklet.
- Ask the participants to read pages two and three of the booklet quietly. Tell them they will have a few minutes to do so (about five minutes).
- Invite them to mark the text when they read something that strikes them.

Share it with others

- Read the reflection on slide 2 and/or the reflection(s) provided in the booklet. Ask participants to discuss these questions in their small groups as a means of applying what they have learned in the text. Encourage them to take notes in their booklets. Give them several minutes to do all this. You may wish to play quiet music in the background during this time.
- If the assembly is large, ask the spokesperson of each small group to share a summary of the group's discussion with the larger group. Write on the board a short version or outline of all the responses.
- Use the PowerPoint slide 3 to provide the group with a visual of a Scripture passage. Open your Bibles to 1 Thessalonians 2:13, and select a few verses to read aloud. How does this Scripture passage relate to what you have just read and discussed?
- Pause for a few moments of silence, then go to the illustration on slide 4, which is also found in the booklet. Ask the participants to look at the illustration. On the back cover you will find a reference for this illustration, from Scripture or the *Catechism*, that may assist you. The Bible is a collection of books written over many years by various human authors, each inspired by God. As we come to know the Bible, we can see it as a "library of books," each book different from the other. Yet all come from the same author, and each one is addressed to us. In what ways is the Bible like a "library"?
- Invite feedback and general conversation about this illustration and its commentary (about five minutes).

Break

Pages four and five

The illustration

- Show the illustration on slide 5, which is the same as the one in the booklet. Invite the participants to look at the illustration. Ask questions such as: Can you relate to this image of a table with books, a pen, a candle? What does this image remind you of? Why?
- Refer to the quote on the back cover. "To compose the sacred books God chose certain people." There are many kinds of literature in Scripture—poetry, history, liturgy, parables, narrative stories, and others. In order to fully understand the texts we must understand what the authors intended to write. Beyond that we need to hear what God is saying to us personally. Do I read the Bible as a personal message to me?
- Invite feedback on this illustration and its commentary (about 5 minutes).

Read and reflect

- Ask participants to read pages four and five. Follow the same process for reading and reflection that you used for the first pages.

Share it with others

- Read the reflection on slide 6 and/or the reflection(s) provided in the booklet. Use the same format for group discussion and sharing as you did for the previous pages.
- Use PowerPoint slide 7 to provide the group with a visual of a Scripture passage. Open your Bibles to Luke 24:45, and select a few verses to read aloud. How does this Scripture passage relate to what you have just read and discussed?
- Pause for a few moments of silence.

Pages six and seven

Personal experience

- Ask everyone to look at the first heading on page six, "The books of the Bible." Invite them to reflect on such questions as: Am I familiar with the contents page of the Bible? Is the Bible a confusing maze of persons and places? Have I ever read the Old Testament books, or even the New Testament, on my own?
- Ask the participants to list as many books of the New Testament as they can.

Read and reflect
- Again, follow the same process for reading and reflection on pages six and seven.

Share it with others
- Read the reflection on slide 8 and/or the reflection(s) provided in the booklet. Use the same format for group discussion and sharing.
- Use PowerPoint slide 9 to provide the group with a visual of a Scripture passage. Open your Bibles to Romans 1:16, and select a few verses to read aloud. How does this Scripture passage relate to what you have just read and discussed?
- Pause for a few moments of silence, then go to the illustration on slide 10, which is the same as the one on these pages. Ask the participants to look at the illustration. Refer to the quote on the back cover. Explain that the Bible was handed down in copies made by monks, painstakingly written out one at a time, until the invention of the printing press in the mid-1400s.

Exercise
- At some point invite the participants to do the exercise on page five of the booklet. The aim is to help them become more familiar with the Bible. When they have all finished, they could share their findings with the others in their small group. If there is not enough time to complete the exercise during the session, encourage the members to do it at home.

Take it home
- Before the end of the evening, ask the small groups to talk once more about how they plan to take home and live what they have learned. Refer to the reflections, and suggest they use them to help apply the core message of this booklet. Invite them to make concrete and realistic plans. Allow a few minutes for this discussion.

Conclusion
- Go to slide 11 and announce the time and place of the next gathering.
- Go to slide 12 and invite everyone to pray the closing prayer aloud. (You can make copies of the prayer, found on page 29 of this guide, or use the prayer of Blessed John XXIII on page 5.) You can, instead, invite the group to offer spontaneous prayer. You may also close the evening with the dismissal song on the CD.

Session Plan for Reflection Booklet **5**

Do You Believe?

Content summary

The response to divine revelation is faith (based on articles 142–184 in the *Catechism of the Catholic Church*)

- Faith is a personal loyalty of our whole being to God who reveals himself to us.
- In order to believe we need the help and gifts of the Holy Spirit.
- Believing is a human act, conscious and free, corresponding to the dignity of the human person.
- Believing is also an ecclesial act. Our belief is stronger because the church guides us and teaches us.

Preparation

- Read through the booklet once, reflectively. Reread it and make your own notes.
- Read through the session plan and become comfortable with the format.
- For more background, read articles 142–184 of the *Catechism*. Mark and look up any unfamiliar words.
- Decide if and when you will do the exercise found after the material for pages six and seven. Have the materials needed.
- See pages 12–13 in this guide for other steps for preparation and materials needed.

Opening

- After introductions, if the number of participants is ten or more, ask them to form small groups. If the assembly is a large one, have each group choose a spokesperson.
- Have PowerPoint slide 1 (the cover illustration) on the screen as you begin.
- Open with the prayer found on page 4 in the introductory section of this guide. You may make copies for the participants. Or use the gathering song on the CD.
- Use the Question of the Week approach to break open the word of God from the Sunday liturgy (see 6 on page 12). Then continue with the *Growing Faith* booklet.

Pages two and three

Read and reflect

- Make sure everyone has a copy of the booklet.
- Ask the participants to read pages two and three of the booklet quietly. Tell them they will have a few minutes to do so (about five minutes).
- Invite them to mark the text when they read something that strikes them.

Share it with others

- Read the reflection on slide 2 and/or the reflection(s) provided in the booklet. Ask participants to discuss these questions in their small groups as a means of applying what they have learned in the text. Encourage them to take notes in their booklets. Give them several minutes to do all this. You may wish to play quiet music in the background during this time.
- If the assembly is large, ask the spokesperson of each small group to share a summary of the group's discussion with the larger group. Write on the board a short version or outline of all the responses.
- Use the PowerPoint slide 3 to provide the group with a visual of a Scripture passage. Open your Bibles to Hebrews 11:8, and select a few verses to read aloud. How does this Scripture passage relate to what you have just read and discussed?
- Pause for a few moments of silence, then go to the illustration on slide 4, which is also found in the booklet. Ask the participants to look at the illustration. On the back cover you will find a reference for this illustration, from Scripture or the *Catechism*, that may assist you. Mary is the model of faith for all of us. She believed in God's promises, even though it meant considerable commitment on her part. She is, indeed, "the faithful one," the first disciple of Jesus. Her faith never wavered. In what ways can I imitate Mary's faith?
- Invite feedback and general conversation about this illustration and its commentary (about five minutes).

Break

Pages four and five

The illustration

- Show slide 5. Invite the participants to look at the illustration, which is the same as the one in the booklet. Ask questions such as: What does the image of light coming through a window mean to you? How might it relate to faith?
- Refer to the quote on the back cover. "Faith makes us taste in advance the light of the beatific vision." We often speak of faith as an "enlightenment." Faith helps us see the truth, and the possibility of love. Faith burns within us like a bright light. We need to keep our eyes open to this light, the light of the Holy Spirit.
- Invite feedback on this illustration and its commentary (about 5 minutes).

Read and reflect

- Ask participants to read pages four and five. Follow the same process for reading and reflection that you used for the first pages.

Share it with others

- Read the reflection on slide 6 and/or the reflection(s) provided in the booklet. Use the same format for group discussion and sharing as you did for the previous pages.
- Use PowerPoint slide 7 to provide the group with a visual of a Scripture passage. Open your Bibles to Matthew 16:17, and select a few verses to read aloud. How does this Scripture passage relate to what you have just read and discussed?
- Pause for a few moments of silence.

Pages six and seven

Personal experience

- Ask everyone to look at the first heading on page six, "Believe freely." Invite them to reflect on these questions: What does "being free" mean to me? What are some areas or practices in my life that show I am a free being? Why is it important to be able to "believe freely"?
- Hand out sheets of blank paper and pencils and ask participants to draw a picture of themselves living their faith freely, or symbols representing freedom.

Read and reflect

- Again, follow the same process for reading and reflection on pages six and seven.

Share it with others

- Read the reflection on slide 8 and/or the reflection(s) provided in the booklet. Use the same format for group discussion and sharing.
- Use PowerPoint slide 9 to provide the group with a visual of a Scripture passage. Open your Bibles to Luke 1:3–4, and select a few verses to read aloud. How does this Scripture passage relate to what you have just read and discussed?
- Pause for a few moments of silence, then go to the illustration on slide 10, which is the same as the one on these pages. Ask the participants to look at the illustration. Refer to the quote on the back cover. Faith is handed on from one generation to the next, a living reality found not in books but in hearts. We are the ones to pass this faith on, to our families, our friends, those whom we minister to, and so on. Each person is free to accept the faith as a free response to God. When we do, we share in the faith of the church, the people of God.

Exercise

- At some point have participants make a list of three specific, concrete ways in which they share or witness to their faith. How do these impact their own lives and the lives of others? If there isn't time for the exercise during this session, encourage them to do it on their own.

Take it home

- Before the end of the evening, ask the small groups to talk once more about how they plan to take home and live what they have learned. Refer to the reflections, and suggest they use them to help apply the core message of this booklet. Invite them to make concrete and realistic plans. Allow a few minutes for this discussion.

Conclusion

- Go to slide 11 and announce the time and place of the next gathering.
- Go to slide 12 and invite everyone to pray the closing prayer aloud. (You can make copies of the prayer, found on page 29 of this guide, or use the prayer of Blessed John XXIII on page 5.) You can, instead, invite the group to offer spontaneous prayer. You may also close the evening with the dismissal song on the CD.

Session Plan for Reflection Booklet **6**

In Whom Do You Believe?

Content summary

The one true God (based on articles 198–231 in the *Catechism of the Catholic Church*)

- God is love.
- God is neither male nor female. God is God.
- God's name is YHWH, which means, I AM.
- Faith helps us see and hear the truth.

Preparation

- Read through the booklet once, reflectively. Reread it and make your own notes.
- Read through the session plan and become comfortable with the format.
- For more background, read articles 198–231 of the *Catechism*. Mark and look up any unfamiliar words.
- Decide if and when you will do the exercise found after the material for pages six and seven. Have the materials needed.
- See pages 12–13 in this Gguide for other steps for preparation and materials needed.

Opening

- After introductions, if the number of participants is ten or more, ask them to form small groups. If the assembly is a large one, have each group choose a spokesperson.
- Have PowerPoint slide 1 (the cover illustration) on the screen as you begin.
- Open with the prayer found on page 4 in the introductory section of this guide. You may make copies for the participants. Or use the gathering song on the CD.
- Use the Question of the Week approach to break open the word of God from the Sunday liturgy (see 6 on page 12). Then continue with the *Growing Faith* booklet.

Pages two and three

Read and reflect

- Make sure everyone has a copy of the booklet.
- Ask the participants to read pages two and three of the booklet quietly. Tell them they will have a few minutes to do so (about five minutes).
- Invite them to mark the text when they read something that strikes them.

Share it with others

- Read the reflection on slide 2 and/or the reflection(s) provided in the booklet. Ask participants to discuss these questions in their small groups as a means of applying what they have learned in the text. Encourage them to take notes in their booklets. Give them several minutes to do all this. You may wish to play quiet music in the background during this time.
- If the assembly is large, ask the spokesperson of each small group to share a summary of the group's discussion with the larger group. Write on the board a short version or outline of all the responses.
- Use the PowerPoint slide 3 to provide the group with a visual of a Scripture passage. Open your Bibles to Exodus 3:14, and select a few verses to read aloud. How does this Scripture passage relate to what you have just read and discussed?
- Pause for a few moments of silence, then go to the illustration on slide 4, which is also found in the booklet. Ask the participants to look at the illustration. On the back cover you will find a reference for this illustration, from Scripture or the *Catechism*, that may assist you. Throughout our human history we have sought to learn more about the God who created us. God revealed the divine name to Moses at the burning bush as a mysterious name, one that leads us deeply into the heart of God: "I am who I am." "Faced with God's fascinating and mysterious presence, [we] discover [our] own insignificance. [In fact] Moses takes off his sandals and veils his face in the presence of God's holiness." (*Catechism*, 208–210).
- Invite feedback about this illustration and its commentary (about five minutes).

Break

Pages four and five

The illustration

- Show the illustration on slide 5, which is the same as the one in the booklet. Invite the participants to look at the illustration. Ask questions such as: What does "I am who am" mean to you? Is this just a theological explanation, or does it affect your daily life? Think of words or a name for God that helps you pray.
- Refer to the quote on the back cover. "In revealing his mysterious name, God says who he is." We all have names for God. What are they? How we call on God is an expression of our own faith. In both the Old and new Testaments God is described with the attributes of a mother (e.g., Isaiah 49:15–16). Jesus teaches us to call God "Father."
- Invite feedback on this illustration and its commentary (about 5 minutes).

Read and reflect

- Ask participants to read pages four and five. Follow the same process for reading and reflection that you used for the first pages.

Share it with others

- Read the reflection on slide 6 and/or the reflection(s) provided in the booklet. Use the same format for group discussion and sharing as you did for the previous pages.
- Use PowerPoint slide 7 to provide the group with a visual of a Scripture passage. Open your Bibles to Exodus 3:5, and select a few verses to read aloud. How does this Scripture passage relate to what you have just read and discussed?
- Pause for a few moments of silence.

Pages six and seven

Personal experience

- Ask everyone to look at the first heading on page six, "God is Love." Invite them to reflect on these questions: Have I experienced real love in my own life? When and with whom? Does my love for another person make me want the best for him or her, even at the cost of personal sacrifice? What does this tell me about God's love?

Read and reflect

- Again, follow the same process for reading and reflection on pages six and seven.

Share it with others

- Read the reflection on slide 8 and/or the reflection(s) provided in the booklet. Use the same format for group discussion and sharing.
- Use PowerPoint slide 9 to provide the group with a visual of a Scripture passage. Open your Bibles to Jeremiah 31:3, and select a few verses to read aloud. How does this Scripture passage relate to what you have just read and discussed?
- Pause for a few moments of silence, then go to the illustration on slide 10, which is the same as the one on these pages. Ask the participants to look at the illustration. Refer to the quote on the back cover. God has assured us that God will always be with us, no matter what. Even if the mountains themselves turn to dust, God will still be at our side. What a wonderful divine promise! How reassuring this is in times of insecurity and lack of commitment. On my part how faithful am I to God?

Exercise

- If time permits, invite participants to do the exercise on page six. It will assist them in exploring the facets of their relationship with God. Another means for discovering which names of God are most familiar and appealing is by writing down favorite Scripture passages. This exercise can be completed at home if there isn't time during the session.

Take it home

- Before the end of the evening, ask the small groups to talk once more about how they plan to take home and live what they have learned. Refer to the reflections, and suggest they use them to help apply the core message of this booklet. Invite them to make concrete and realistic plans. Allow a few minutes for this discussion.

Conclusion

- Go to slide 11 and announce the time and place of the next gathering.
- Go to slide 12 and invite everyone to pray the closing prayer aloud. (You can make copies of the prayer, found on page 29 of this guide, or use the prayer of Blessed John XXIII on page 5.) You can, instead, invite the group to offer spontaneous prayer. You may also close the evening with the dismissal song on the CD.

Session Plan for Reflection Booklet 7

What Is the Love of the Trinity?

Content summary

God is one in three (based on articles 232–267 in the *Catechism of the Catholic Church*)

- We believe in one God.
- God alone is the origin of life and our ultimate goal.
- Even when God reveals God's self, God remains a mystery beyond words.
- The mystery of the Trinity is the central Christian mystery. God is three in one: Father, Son, and Holy Spirit.

Preparation

- Read through the booklet once, reflectively. Reread it and make your own notes.
- Read through the session plan and become comfortable with the format.
- For more background, read articles 232–267 of the *Catechism*. Mark and look up any unfamiliar words.
- Decide if and when you will do the exercise found after the material for pages six and seven. Have the materials needed.
- See pages 12–13 in this guide for other steps for preparation and materials needed.

Opening

- After introductions, if the number of participants is ten or more, ask them to form small groups. If the assembly is a large one, have each group choose a spokesperson.
- Have PowerPoint slide 1 (the cover illustration) on the screen as you begin.
- Open with the prayer found on page 4 in the introductory section of this guide. You may make copies for the participants. Or use the gathering song on the CD.
- Use the Question of the Week approach to break open the word of God from the Sunday liturgy (see 6 on page 12). Then continue with the *Growing Faith* booklet.

Pages two and three

Read and reflect

- Make sure everyone has a copy of the booklet.
- Ask the participants to read pages two and three of the booklet quietly. Tell them they will have a few minutes to do so (about five minutes).
- Invite them to mark the text when they read something that strikes them.

Share it with others

- Read the reflection on slide 2 and/or the reflection(s) provided in the booklet. Ask participants to discuss these questions in their small groups as a means of applying what they have learned in the text. Encourage them to take notes in their booklets. Give them several minutes to do all this. You may wish to play quiet music in the background during this time.
- If the assembly is large, ask the spokesperson of each small group to share a summary of the group's discussion with the larger group. Write on the board a short version or outline of all the responses.
- Use the PowerPoint slide 3 to provide the group with a visual of a Scripture passage. Open your Bibles to Matthew 28:19, and select a few verses to read aloud. How does this Scripture passage relate to what you have just read and discussed?
- Pause for a few moments of silence, then go to the illustration on slide 4, which is also found in the booklet. Ask the participants to look at the illustration. On the back cover you will find a reference for this illustration, from Scripture or the *Catechism*, that may assist you. We believe that God is three Persons in one God, just as this lily is three blossoms on one stem. God is one God, not three. "God has left traces of his Trinitarian being in his work of creation and in his Revelation throughout the Old Testament. But his inmost being as Holy Trinity is a mystery that is inaccessible to reason alone or even to Israel's faith before the Incarnation of God's Son and the sending of the Holy Spirit" (*Catechism*, 237).
- Invite feedback and general conversation about this illustration and its commentary (about five minutes).

Break

Pages four and five

The illustration

- Show the illustration on slide 5, which is the same as the one in the booklet. Invite the participants to look at the illustration. Ask questions such as: Can you relate to this image of the door? Is it mysterious? Inviting? The sign of a special place? How might it relate to the mystery of the Trinity?
- Write or draw a description of what or who you think might be on the other side of the door.
- Refer to the quote on the back cover. "Make [my soul] your heaven, your beloved dwelling." God provides us with "doorways to the sacred" through which we go together to find God together. Indeed, God draws us in. For us Catholics some of the doorways through which we encounter God are the sacraments. Can you name other doorways?
- Invite feedback on this illustration and its commentary (about 5 minutes).

Read and reflect

- Ask participants to read pages four and five. Follow the same process for reading and reflection that you used for the first pages.

Share it with others

- Read the reflection on slide 6 and/or the reflection(s) provided in the booklet. Use the same format for group discussion and sharing as you did for the previous pages.
- Use PowerPoint slide 7 to provide the group with a visual of a Scripture passage. Open your Bibles to Ephesians 1:1, and select a few verses to read aloud. How does this Scripture passage relate to what you have just read and discussed?
- Pause for a few moments of silence.

Pages six and seven

Personal experience

- Ask everyone to look at the first heading on page six, "One God." Invite them to reflect on these questions: What concrete effect does my belief in the holy Trinity have on my daily life (at home, at work, in times of relaxation) and on my attitudes toward other people? Explain.

Read and reflect

- Again, follow the same process for reading and reflection on pages six and seven.

Share it with others

- Read the reflection on slide 8 and/or the reflection(s) provided in the booklet. Use the same format for group discussion and sharing.
- Use PowerPoint slide 9 to provide the group with a visual of a Scripture passage. Open your Bibles to John 17:21, and select a few verses to read aloud. How does this Scripture passage relate to what you have just read and discussed?
- Pause for a few moments of silence, then go to slide 10. Ask the participants to look at the illustration, which is the same as the one on these pages. Refer to the quote on the back cover. Whenever we come together in the spirit of God, we can be sure Christ is present among us. One of the ways we come to understand about God is by reflection on these moments of "togetherness." They are sacred gatherings. Name some times when we gather, whether for religious purposes, as a family, for work, and so on.

Exercise

- Invite the participants to complete the exercise on page two. The ways Jesus refers to God can give us a deeper insight into the mystery of God. Encourage the members to take time at home to write some of their own metaphors, images, or a parable to refer to God.

Take it home

- Before the end of the evening, ask the small groups to talk once more about how they plan to take home and live what they have learned. Refer to the reflections, and suggest they use them to help apply the core message of this booklet. Invite them to make concrete and realistic plans. Allow a few minutes for this discussion.

Conclusion

- Go to slide 11 and announce the time and place of the next gathering.
- Go to slide 12 and invite everyone to pray the closing prayer aloud. (You can make copies of the prayer, found on page 29 of this guide, or use the prayer of Blessed John XXIII on page 5.) You can, instead, invite the group to offer spontaneous prayer. You may also close the evening with the dismissal song on the CD.

Session Plan for Reflection Booklet **8**

How Did God Create the World?

Content summary

God the Creator (based on articles 268–324 in the *Catechism of the Catholic Church*)

- In the creation of the world and of us, God gave the first and universal witness to God's almighty love and wisdom.
- God alone created the universe freely, directly, and without any help.
- God created the universe and keeps it in existence through Jesus Christ, in whom all things continue in being, and by the Spirit, the giver of life.
- The fact that physical and moral evil exists is a mystery.

Preparation

- Read through the booklet once, reflectively. Reread it and make your own notes.
- Read through the session plan and become comfortable with the format.
- For more background, read articles 268–324 of the *Catechism*. Mark and look up any unfamiliar words.
- Decide if and when you will do the exercise found after the material for pages six and seven. Have the materials needed.
- See pages 12–13 in this guide for other steps for preparation and materials needed.

Opening

- After introductions, if the number of participants is ten or more, ask them to form small groups. If the assembly is a large one, have each group choose a spokesperson.
- Have PowerPoint slide 1 (the cover illustration) on the screen as you begin.
- Open with the prayer found on page 4 in the introductory section of this guide. You may make copies for the participants. Or use the gathering song on the CD.
- Use the Question of the Week approach to break open the word of God from the Sunday liturgy (see 6 on page 12). Then continue with the *Growing Faith* booklet.

Pages two and three

Read and reflect

- Make sure everyone has a copy of the booklet.
- Ask the participants to read pages two and three of the booklet quietly. Tell them they will have a few minutes to do so (about five minutes).
- Invite them to mark the text when they read something that strikes them.

Share it with others

- Read the reflection on slide 2 and/or the reflection(s) provided in the booklet. Ask participants to discuss these questions in their small groups as a means of applying what they have learned in the text. Encourage them to take notes in their booklets. Give them several minutes to do all this. You may wish to play quiet music in the background during this time.
- If the assembly is large, ask the spokesperson of each small group to share a summary of the group's discussion with the larger group. Write on the board a short version or outline of all the responses.
- Use the PowerPoint slide 3 to provide the group with a visual of a Scripture passage. Open your Bibles to Genesis 1:10, and select a few verses to read aloud. How does this Scripture passage relate to what you have just read and discussed?
- Pause for a few moments of silence, then go to the illustration on slide 4, which is also found in the booklet. Ask the participants to look at the illustration. On the back cover you will find a reference for this illustration, from Scripture or the *Catechism*, that may assist you. We humans use science to study our world and ourselves. This study is not in conflict with our faith, but in fact, supports it and can also be a way to participate in God's creative work. Through a better knowledge of creation, we also draw closer to the Creator.
- Invite feedback and general conversation about this illustration and its commentary (about five minutes).

Break

Pages four and five

The illustration

- Show the illustration on slide 5, which is the same as the one in the booklet. Invite the participants to look at the illustration. Ask questions such as: What does the image of the field remind you of? Close your eyes and go back to the memories this image evokes.
- Refer to the quote on the back cover. "For you [God] love all things that exist." God is creator of all things. As we observe creation around us, we see God's handiwork. This field of grass, ordinary as it seems, is a sign of the divine love and care for us.
- Invite feedback on this illustration and its commentary (about 5 minutes).

Read and reflect

- Ask participants to read pages four and five. Follow the same process for reading and reflection that you used for the first pages.

Share it with others

- Read the reflection on slide 6 and/or the reflection(s) provided in the booklet. Use the same format for group discussion and sharing as you did for the previous pages.
- Use PowerPoint slide 7 to provide the group with a visual of a Scripture passage. Open your Bibles to Genesis 1:1, and select a few verses to read aloud. How does this Scripture passage relate to what you have just read and discussed?
- Pause for a few moments of silence.

Pages six and seven

Personal experience

- Ask everyone to look at the second heading on page six, "Evil." Invite them to reflect on these questions: What does the word "evil" mean to me? What kinds of evil have I experienced in my life? Was it hard to understand the reason for it? Whom did I turn to?

Read and reflect

- Again, follow the same process for reading and reflection on pages six and seven.

Share it with others

- Read the reflection on slide 8 and/or the reflection(s) provided in the booklet. Use the same format for group discussion and sharing.
- Use PowerPoint slide 9 to provide the group with a visual of a Scripture passage. Open your Bibles to Genesis 50:20, and select a few verses to read aloud. How does this Scripture passage relate to what you have just read and discussed?
- Pause for a few moments of silence, then go to the illustration on slide 10, which is the same as the one on these pages. Ask the participants to look at the illustration. Refer to the quote on the back cover. Talk about the fact that every created material thing turns to dust. No matter how beautiful the creation is, decay is part of life. We carry our treasure in jars of clay, St. Paul wrote. We ourselves grow old. Our bodies die, but we live on in the spirit. Because we are limited we sometimes make choices that hurt ourselves and others.

Exercise

- Give each group a set of markers and some pencils, and each participant a sheet of white paper. Ask everyone to draw an expression of what creation means to them. It can be a picture or just a dash of color—whatever they are inspired to do. Encourage them to share their drawings with the others in their group.

Take it home

- Before the end of the evening, ask the small groups to talk once more about how they plan to take home and live what they have learned. Refer to the reflections, and suggest they use them to help apply the core message of this booklet. Invite them to make concrete and realistic plans. Allow a few minutes for this discussion.

Conclusion

- Go to slide 11 and announce the time and place of the next gathering.
- Go to slide 12 and invite everyone to pray the closing prayer aloud. (You can make copies of the prayer, found on page 29 of this guide, or use the prayer of Blessed John XXIII on page 5.) You can, instead, invite the group to offer spontaneous prayer. You may also close the evening with the dismissal song on the CD.

Session Plan for Reflection Booklet **9**

How Are We in God's Image?

Content summary

God creates everything seen and unseen (based on articles 325–373 in the *Catechism of the Catholic Church*)

- Angels are God's messengers and our protectors.
- God willed the diversity of creatures and their own particular goodness, their interdependence, and their order.
- God destined all material creatures for the good of the human race.
- We humans are a unity of body and soul.

Preparation

- Read through the booklet once, reflectively. Reread it and make your own notes.
- Read through the session plan and become comfortable with the format.
- For more background, read articles 325–373 of the *Catechism*. Mark and look up any unfamiliar words.
- Decide if and when you will do the exercise found after the material for pages six and seven. Have the materials needed.
- See pages 12–13 in this guide for other steps for preparation and materials needed.

Opening

- After introductions, if the number of participants is ten or more, ask them to form small groups. If the assembly is a large one, have each group choose a spokesperson.
- Have PowerPoint slide 1 (the cover illustration) on the screen as you begin.
- Open with the prayer found on page 4 in the introductory section of this guide. You may make copies for the participants. Or use the gathering song on the CD.
- Use the Question of the Week approach to break open the word of God from the Sunday liturgy (see 6 on page 12). Then continue with the *Growing Faith* booklet.

Pages two and three

Read and reflect

- Make sure everyone has a copy of the booklet.
- Ask the participants to read pages two and three of the booklet quietly. Tell them they will have a few minutes to do so (about five minutes).
- Invite them to mark the text when they read something that strikes them.

Share it with others

- Read the reflection on slide 2 and/or the reflection(s) provided in the booklet. Ask participants to discuss these questions in their small groups as a means of applying what they have learned in the text. Encourage them to take notes in their booklets. Give them several minutes to do all this. You may wish to play quiet music in the background during this time.
- If the assembly is large, ask the spokesperson of each small group to share a summary of the group's discussion with the larger group. Write on the board a short version or outline of all the responses.
- Use the PowerPoint slide 3 to provide the group with a visual of a Scripture passage. Open your Bibles to Genesis 1:29–30, and select a few verses to read aloud. How does this Scripture passage relate to what you have just read and discussed?
- Pause for a few moments of silence, then go to the illustration on slide 4, which is also found in the booklet. Ask the participants to look at the illustration. On the back cover you will find a reference for this illustration, from Scripture or the *Catechism*, that may assist you. We are all responsible for the care of the earth, including animals, plants, minerals, air, and water. Like this girl washing her cow, we are all accountable for caring for creation. This involves more than just caring for the things we own or have in our control. We also need to take action to protect our environment, endangered species and land, and abused peoples and animals.
- Invite feedback and general conversation about this illustration and its commentary (about five minutes).

Break

Pages four and five

The illustration

- Show the illustration on slide 5, which is the same as the one in the booklet. Invite the participants to look at the illustration. Ask questions such as: What does this group of people make you think of? Look carefully at their faces. What do they tell you? How often do you look into the face of another person and see God's image there? Even if it is soiled, or bleary-eyed from drugs or alcohol, or a different color from yours?
- Refer to the quote on the back cover. "God created humankind in his image...." God desires all women and men to live together in peace. "Created in his image" does not exclude anyone, regardless of race, religion, ethnic background, or condition in life. Each person is to be treated with dignity. The goods of the earth are meant to be shared by all, not hoarded by the few.
- Invite feedback on this illustration and its commentary (about 5 minutes).

Read and reflect

- Ask participants to read pages four and five. Follow the same process for reading and reflection that you used for the first pages.

Share it with others

- Read the reflection on slide 6 and/or the reflection(s) provided in the booklet. Use the same format for group discussion and sharing as you did for the previous pages.
- Use PowerPoint slide 7 to provide the group with a visual of a Scripture passage. Open your Bibles to Genesis 1:28, and select a few verses to read aloud. How does this Scripture passage relate to what you have just read and discussed?
- Pause for a few moments of silence.

Pages six and seven

Personal experience

- Ask everyone to look at the first heading on page six, "Two accounts." Invite them to reflect on these questions: When two or more people witness an event or place, will each one describe it the same way as the other persons do? What would make each account different?

- Hand out sheets of blank paper and pencils and ask everyone to write a brief description of your meeting space, then share their descriptions with their groups.

Read and reflect

- Again, follow the same process for reading and reflection on pages six and seven.

Share it with others

- Read the reflection on slide 8 and/or the reflection(s) provided in the booklet. Use the same format for group discussion and sharing.
- Use PowerPoint slide 9 to provide the group with a visual of a Scripture passage. Open your Bibles to Wisdom 11:24, and select a few verses to read aloud. How does this Scripture passage relate to what you have just read and discussed?
- Pause for a few moments of silence, then go to the illustration on slide 10, which is the same as the one on these pages. Ask the participants to look at the illustration. Refer to the quote on the back cover. Spending time outdoors with nature and creation is good for us and part of the pathway to holiness. We tend to rush from activity to activity, not pausing often enough to drink in the beauty around us. Because of this we miss the chance to see God's work and presence among us.

Exercise

- Invite everyone to write down some concrete ways in which they show respect for God's creation: people, animals, nature; then write some areas in which they could improve. Those who wish can share what they wrote with the rest of their group.

Take it home

- Before the end of the evening, ask the small groups to talk once more about how they plan to take home and live what they have learned. Refer to the reflections, and suggest they use them to help apply the core message of this booklet. Invite them to make concrete and realistic plans. Allow a few minutes for this discussion.

Conclusion

- Go to slide 11 and announce the time and place of the next gathering.
- Go to slide 12 and invite everyone to pray the closing prayer aloud. (You can make copies of the prayer, found on page 29 of this guide, or use the prayer of Blessed John XXIII on page 5.) You can, instead, invite the group to offer spontaneous prayer. You may also close the evening with the dismissal song on the CD.

Session Plan for Reflection Booklet **10**

Why Do People Turn Away from God?

Content summary

The reality of sin and grace (based on articles 374–421 in the *Catechism of the Catholic Church*)

- We were created to live in paradise and be near God.
- From the beginning we humans have experienced an inclination to be selfish and unilateral. This is called "original sin."
- As a result of original sin, human nature is weakened and inclined to sin.
- Everyone experiences original sin.

Preparation

- Read through the booklet once, reflectively. Reread it and make your own notes.
- Read through the session plan and become comfortable with the format.
- For more background, read articles 374–421 of the *Catechism*. Mark and look up any unfamiliar words.
- Decide if and when you will do the exercise found after the material for pages six and seven. Have the materials needed.
- See pages 12–13 in this guide for other steps for preparation and materials needed.

Opening

- After introductions, if the number of participants is ten or more, ask them to form small groups. If the assembly is a large one, have each group choose a spokesperson.
- Have PowerPoint slide 1 (the cover illustration) on the screen as you begin.
- Open with the prayer found on page 4 in the introductory section of this guide. You may make copies for the participants. Or use the gathering song on the CD.
- Use the Question of the Week approach to break open the word of God from the Sunday liturgy (see 6 on page 12). Then continue with the *Growing Faith* booklet.

Pages two and three

Read and reflect

- Make sure everyone has a copy of the booklet.
- Ask the participants to read pages two and three of the booklet quietly. Tell them they will have a few minutes to do so (about five minutes).
- Invite them to mark the text when they read something that strikes them.

Share it with others

- Read the reflection on slide 2 and/or the reflection(s) provided in the booklet. Ask participants to discuss these questions in their small groups as a means of applying what they have learned in the text. Encourage them to take notes in their booklets. Give them several minutes to do all this. You may wish to play quiet music in the background during this time.
- If the assembly is large, ask the spokesperson of each small group to share a summary of the group's discussion with the larger group. Write on the board a short version or outline of all the responses.
- Use the PowerPoint slide 3 to provide the group with a visual of a Scripture passage. Open your Bibles to Genesis 1:31, and select a few verses to read aloud. How does this Scripture passage relate to what you have just read and discussed?
- Pause for a few moments of silence, then go to the illustration on slide 4, which is also found in the booklet. Ask the participants to look at the illustration. On the back cover you will find a reference for this illustration, from Scripture or the *Catechism*, that may assist you. When we sin, we may find ourselves plunged into darkness and sorrow. We choose what is selfish rather than what is loving and generous. Like this young person we may be weighed down by guilt. Selfish choices go against our created natures as human beings. We were created to live in love, holiness, and harmony with God and creation. When we prefer ourselves to God, we turn away from God.
- Invite feedback about this illustration and its commentary (about five minutes).

Break

Pages four and five

The illustration

- Show the illustration on slide 5, which is the same as the one in the booklet. Invite the participants to look at the illustration. Ask questions such as: Have you ever seen a fountain? What does this image say to you? What do fountains provide? Where in the gospels do we find references to fountains or wells or springs of water? How does God's love continually flow like the water in a fountain?

- Refer to the quote on the back cover. "Jesus said to her, 'Those who drink of the water that I will give them will never be thirsty.'" In our human weakness we look to God for strength and guidance. Christ promised that when we know him, we will be filled with "living water." It will gush up within us like this fountain, a source of life for us.

- Invite feedback on this illustration and its commentary (about 5 minutes).

Read and reflect

- Ask participants to read pages four and five. Follow the same process for reading and reflection that you used for the first pages.

Share it with others

- Read the reflection on slide 6 and/or the reflection(s) provided in the booklet. Use the same format for group discussion and sharing as you did for the previous pages.

- Use PowerPoint slide 7 to provide the group with a visual of a Scripture passage. Open your Bibles to John 1:5, and select a few verses to read aloud. How does this Scripture passage relate to what you have just read and discussed?

- Pause for a few moments of silence.

Pages six and seven

Personal experience

- Ask everyone to look at the first heading on page six, "Hope." Invite them to reflect on these questions: When and for what reason have I needed hope during my life? Have I ever given up or come close to giving up? What or who kept me going?

Read and reflect

- Again, follow the same process for reading and reflection on pages six and seven.

Share it with others

- Read the reflection on slide 8 and/or the reflection(s) provided in the booklet. Use the same format for group discussion and sharing.
- Use PowerPoint slide 9 to provide the group with a visual of a Scripture passage. Open your Bibles to Romans 5:20, and select a few verses to read aloud. How does this Scripture passage relate to what you have just read and discussed?
- Pause for a few moments of silence, then go to the illustration on slide 10, which is the same as the one on these pages. Ask the participants to look at the illustration. Refer to the quote on the back cover. The word "paradise" means garden. The garden can be a symbol of hope, of oneness with a loving God who, despite our failings, continually invites us back to life and love with him. A garden is, generally, a place of peace and harmony, where we can listen to God and be healed.

Exercise

- Provide each person with paper and pencil to do the exercise on page two. Making the two lists is an effective way of assisting participants to connect their faith to situations in their lives and in the world. This exercise also helps raise awareness of the existence of evil in the world, which can be overcome by God's grace.

Take it home

- Before the end of the evening, ask the small groups to talk once more about how they plan to take home and live what they have learned. Refer to the reflections, and suggest they use them to help apply the core message of this booklet. Invite them to make concrete and realistic plans. Allow a few minutes for this discussion.

Conclusion

- Go to slide 11 and announce the time and place of the next gathering.
- Go to slide 12 and invite everyone to pray the closing prayer aloud. (You can make copies of the prayer, found on page 29 of this guide, or use the prayer of Blessed John XXIII on page 5.) You can, instead, invite the group to offer spontaneous prayer. You may also close the evening with the dismissal song on the CD.

Session Plan for Reflection Booklet **11**

Who Do People Say That I Am?

Content summary

You are the Messiah (based on articles 422–483 in the *Catechism of the Catholic Church*)

- The name Jesus means "God saves."
- The title "Christ" means "Anointed One" or Messiah.
- Jesus Christ is true God and true man, in the unity of his divine person, God incarnate.
- The Incarnation is the mystery of the wonderful union of the divine and human natures in the one person of the Son of God.

Preparation

- Read through the booklet once, reflectively. Reread it and make your own notes.
- Read through the session plan and become comfortable with the format.
- For more background, read articles 422–483 of the *Catechism*. Mark and look up any unfamiliar words.
- Decide if and when you will do the exercise found after the material for pages six and seven. Have the materials needed.
- See pages 12–13 in this guide for other steps for preparation and materials needed.

Opening

- After introductions, if the number of participants is ten or more, ask them to form small groups. If the assembly is a large one, have each group choose a spokesperson.
- Have PowerPoint slide 1 (the cover illustration) on the screen as you begin.
- Open with the prayer found on page 4 in the introductory section of this guide. You may make copies for the participants. Or use the gathering song on the CD.
- Use the Question of the Week approach to break open the word of God from the Sunday liturgy (see 6 on page 12). Then continue with the *Growing Faith* booklet.

Pages two and three

Read and reflect

- Make sure everyone has a copy of the booklet.
- Ask the participants to read pages two and three of the booklet quietly. Tell them they will have a few minutes to do so (about five minutes).
- Invite them to mark the text when they read something that strikes them.

Share it with others

- Read the reflection on slide 2 and/or the reflection(s) provided in the booklet. Ask participants to discuss these questions in their small groups as a means of applying what they have learned in the text. Encourage them to take notes in their booklets. Give them several minutes to do all this. You may wish to play quiet music in the background during this time.
- If the assembly is large, ask the spokesperson of each small group to share a summary of the group's discussion with the larger group. Write on the board a short version or outline of all the responses.
- Use the PowerPoint slide 3 to provide the group with a visual of a Scripture passage. Open your Bibles to 1 John 1:3, and select a few verses to read aloud. How does this Scripture passage relate to what you have just read and discussed?
- Pause for a few moments of silence, then go to the illustration on slide 4, which is also found in the booklet. Ask the participants to look at the illustration. On the back cover you will find a reference for this illustration, from Scripture or the *Catechism*, that may assist you. God loves us with the kind of love that a father has for his daughter or son, a desire to teach us and care for us, to protect us and have us near. The love of a parent is often a metaphor telling us how God loves us. Because of this love for us, the parent or family member wants the child to know God, to know Christ—not just intellectually but as a person.
- Invite feedback about this illustration and its commentary (about five minutes).

Break

Pages four and five

The illustration

- Show the illustration on slide 5, which is the same as the one in the booklet. Invite the participants to look at the illustration. Ask questions such as: Pretend you have never heard these words from the gospel before. You are reading them for the first time, as words Jesus spoke to all his followers. What do they mean to you personally? What do they tell you about Jesus? About yourself?
- Refer to the quote on the back cover. "Jesus is the model for the Beatitudes and the norm of the new law [of love]." The words from Matthew 25 set the stage for how we are to live our Christian life. The teachings of Christ lead us to care for those whom we hold dear. By loving others as Jesus did we proclaim with our lives that Jesus is Lord!
- Invite feedback on this illustration and its commentary (about 5 minutes).

Read and reflect

- Ask participants to read pages four and five. Follow the same process for reading and reflection that you used for the first pages.

Share it with others

- Read the reflection on slide 6 and/or the reflection(s) provided in the booklet. Use the same format for group discussion and sharing as you did for the previous pages.
- Use PowerPoint slide 7 to provide the group with a visual of a Scripture passage. Open your Bibles to Matthew 20:28, and select a few verses to read aloud. How does this Scripture passage relate to what you have just read and discussed?
- Pause for a few moments of silence.

Pages six and seven

Personal experience

- Ask everyone to look at the second heading on page six, "The incarnation." Invite them to reflect on these questions: What does the word 'incarnation' mean to me personally—not as a theological explanation but as something real that affects my life? What difference has the life of Christ made in the world, in my world, in my life?

Read and reflect
- Again, follow the same process for reading and reflection on pages six and seven.

Share it with others
- Read the reflection on slide 8 and/or the reflection(s) provided in the booklet. Use the same format for group discussion and sharing.
- Use PowerPoint slide 9 to provide the group with a visual of a Scripture passage. Open your Bibles to John 3:16, and select a few verses to read aloud. How does this Scripture passage relate to what you have just read and discussed?
- Pause for a few moments of silence, then go to the illustration on slide 10, which is the same as the one on these pages. Ask the participants to look at the illustration. Refer to the quote on the back cover. Jesus began his ministry after John baptized him in the Jordan River. John had foretold Jesus' coming. He said, "I baptize you with water…. He will baptize you with the Holy Spirit and fire" (Luke 3:16).

Exercise
- Invite the participants to complete the steps as proposed in the exercise on page six. They are asked to write out in a few lines their own central beliefs about Jesus Christ. In this activity they have the opportunity to clarify and affirm what they believe about the Son of God who became one of us.

Take it home
- Before the end of the evening, ask the small groups to talk once more about how they plan to take home and live what they have learned. Refer to the reflections, and suggest they use them to help apply the core message of this booklet. Invite them to make concrete and realistic plans. Allow a few minutes for this discussion.

Conclusion
- Go to slide 11 and announce the time and place of the next gathering.
- Go to slide 12 and invite everyone to pray the closing prayer aloud. (You can make copies of the prayer, found on page 29 of this guide, or use the prayer of Blessed John XXIII on page 5.) You can, instead, invite the group to offer spontaneous prayer. You may also close the evening with the dismissal song on the CD.

Session Plan for Reflection Booklet **12**

Why Do We Honor Mary?

Content summary

Mary is the Mother of God and Mother of the Church (based on articles 484–511 and 963–975 in the *Catechism of the Catholic Church*)

- Mary is truly "Mother of God," Theotokos.
- With her whole being Mary is "the handmaid of the Lord."
- By pronouncing her "fiat" at the Annunciation and giving her consent to the Incarnation, Mary was already collaborating with the work her Son was to accomplish.
- Mary is now with God where she already shares in the glory of her Son's resurrection, anticipating the resurrection of all.

Preparation

- Read through the booklet once, reflectively. Reread it and make your own notes.
- Read through the session plan and become comfortable with the format.
- For more background, read articles 484–511 and 963–975 of the *Catechism*. Mark and look up any unfamiliar words.
- Decide if and when you will do the exercise found after the material for pages six and seven. Have the materials needed.
- See pages 12–13 in this guide for other steps for preparation and materials needed.

Opening

- After introductions, if the number of participants is ten or more, ask them to form small groups. If the assembly is a large one, have each group choose a spokesperson.
- Have PowerPoint slide 1 (the cover illustration) on the screen as you begin.
- Open with the prayer found on page 4 in the introductory section of this guide. You may make copies for the participants. Or use the gathering song on the CD.
- Use the Question of the Week approach to break open the word of God from the Sunday liturgy (see 6 on page 12). Then continue with the *Growing Faith* booklet.

Pages two and three

Read and reflect

- Make sure everyone has a copy of the booklet.
- Ask the participants to read pages two and three of the booklet quietly. Tell them they will have a few minutes to do so (about five minutes).
- Invite them to mark the text when they read something that strikes them.

Share it with others

- Read the reflection on slide 2 and/or the reflection(s) provided in the booklet. Ask participants to discuss these questions in their small groups as a means of applying what they have learned in the text. Encourage them to take notes in their booklets. Give them several minutes to do all this. You may wish to play quiet music in the background during this time.
- If the assembly is large, ask the spokesperson of each small group to share a summary of the group's discussion with the larger group. Write on the board a short version or outline of all the responses.
- Use the PowerPoint slide 3 to provide the group with a visual of a Scripture passage. Open your Bibles to Luke 1:38, and select a few verses to read aloud. How does this Scripture passage relate to what you have just read and discussed?
- Pause for a few moments of silence, then go to the illustration on slide 4, which is also found in the booklet. Ask the participants to look at the illustration. On the back cover you will find a reference for this illustration, from Scripture or the *Catechism*, that may assist you. When Mary was invited by God to accept her role in salvation history, she did not hesitate. She offered her entire self with these simple words: "(Adsum—) Here am I, the servant of the Lord; let it be with me according to your word" (Luke 1:38). How do we respond when we are called?
- Invite feedback and general conversation about this illustration and its commentary (about five minutes).

Break

Pages four and five

The illustration

- Show the illustration on slide 5, which is the same as the one in the booklet. Invite the participants to look at the illustration. Ask questions such as: Can you relate to this image? One woman is welcoming another; both are filled with new life. What does this image mean to you personally?

- Refer to the quote on the back cover. "Mary is acclaimed by Elizabeth…as 'the mother of my Lord'." Elizabeth's son, John the Baptist, was the last prophet of the Old Testament. Mary's son Jesus inaugurated the reign of God. In this unique and lovely moment, Jesus and John meet while still within the wombs of their mothers. Neither Elizabeth nor Mary fully realized the impact their sons would have on the history of the world or the salvation of all peoples. But their faith in God led them to accept his plan.

- Invite feedback on this illustration and its commentary (about 5 minutes).

Read and reflect

- Ask participants to read pages four and five. Follow the same process for reading and reflection that you used for the first pages.

Share it with others

- Read the reflection on slide 6 and/or the reflection(s) provided in the booklet. Use the same format for group discussion and sharing as you did for the previous pages.

- Use PowerPoint slide 7 to provide the group with a visual of a Scripture passage. Open your Bibles to Luke 1:41, and select a few verses to read aloud. How does this Scripture passage relate to what you have just read and discussed?

- Pause for a few moments of silence.

Pages six and seven

Personal experience

- Ask everyone to look at the first heading on page six, "Mother of the Church." Invite them to reflect on these questions: What do these words mean to me, personally? Some of Mary's titles can seem to remove her from us, from our lives, if we think of them only from their theological perspective. As a member of a domestic church, as a member of the local church and the universal church, how does Mary's role as Mother impact my daily life?

Read and reflect

- Again, follow the same process for reading and reflection on pages six and seven.

Share it with others

- Read the reflection on slide 8 and/or the reflection(s) provided in the booklet. Use the same format for group discussion and sharing.
- Use PowerPoint slide 9 to provide the group with a visual of a Scripture passage. Open your Bibles to Luke 1:48b, and select a few verses to read aloud. How does this Scripture passage relate to what you have just read and discussed?
- Pause for a few moments of silence, then ask the participants to look at the illustration on slide 10, which is the same as the one on these pages. Refer to the quote on the back cover. These words of Mary, which are part of the Hail Mary, come right from the gospels. We pray them and honor Mary because of her faithfulness, openness to God's will, and holiness. "By her complete adherence to the Father's will, to his Son's redemptive work, and to every prompting of the Holy Spirit, the Virgin Mary is the Church's model of faith and charity" (*Catechism*, 967).

Exercise

- If possible, play the song by Paul McCartney, *Let It Be*. Then invite the participants to write their own poem, prayer, or expression of praise in honor of Mary's "Yes" to God.

Take it home

- Before the end of the evening, ask the small groups to talk once more about how they plan to take home and live what they have learned. Refer to the reflections, and suggest they use them to help apply the core message of this booklet. Invite them to make concrete and realistic plans. Allow a few minutes for this discussion.

Conclusion

- Go to slide 11 and announce the time and place of the next gathering.
- Go to slide 12 and invite everyone to pray the closing prayer aloud. (You can make copies of the prayer, found on page 29 of this guide, or use the prayer of Blessed John XXIII on page 5.) You can, instead, invite the group to offer spontaneous prayer. You may also close the evening with the dismissal song on the CD.

Session Plan for Reflection Booklet **13**

What Did Christ Teach?

Content summary

The reign of God (based on articles 512–570 in the *Catechism of the Catholic Church*)
- The whole of Christ's life was a continual teaching: his silence, his miracles, his gestures, his prayer, his love for people, his special affection for the little and the poor, his way of the cross, and his resurrection.
- In his teaching, Jesus announced the reign of God.
- Jesus fulfilled the law with such perfection that he revealed its ultimate meaning.
- We are called to live out the paschal mystery as Christ did.

Preparation

- Read through the booklet once, reflectively. Reread it and make your own notes.
- Read through the session plan and become comfortable with the format.
- For more background, read articles 512–570 of the *Catechism*. Mark and look up any unfamiliar words.
- Decide if and when you will do the exercise found after the material for pages six and seven. Have the materials needed.
- See pages 12–13 in this guide for other steps for preparation and materials needed.

Opening

- After introductions, if the number of participants is ten or more, ask them to form small groups. If the assembly is a large one, have each group choose a spokesperson.
- Have PowerPoint slide 1 (the cover illustration) on the screen as you begin.
- Open with the prayer found on page 4 in the introductory section of this guide. You may make copies for the participants. Or use the gathering song on the CD.
- Use the Question of the Week approach to break open the word of God from the Sunday liturgy (see 6 on page 12). Then continue with the *Growing Faith* booklet.

Pages two and three

Read and reflect

- Make sure everyone has a copy of the booklet.
- Ask the participants to read pages two and three of the booklet quietly. Tell them they will have a few minutes to do so (about five minutes).
- Invite them to mark the text when they read something that strikes them.

Share it with others

- Read the reflection on slide 2 and/or the reflection(s) provided in the booklet. Ask participants to discuss these questions in their small groups as a means of applying what they have learned in the text. Encourage them to take notes in their booklets. Give them several minutes to do all this. You may wish to play quiet music in the background during this time.
- If the assembly is large, ask the spokesperson of each small group to share a summary of the group's discussion with the larger group. Write on the board a short version or outline of all the responses.
- Use the PowerPoint slide 3 to provide the group with a visual of a Scripture passage. Open your Bibles to Luke 22:14, 19b, and select a few verses to read aloud. How does this Scripture passage relate to what you have just read and discussed?
- Pause for a few moments of silence, then go to the illustration on slide 4, which is also found in the booklet. Ask the participants to look at the illustration. On the back cover you will find a reference for this illustration, from Scripture or the *Catechism*, that may assist you. Gathering for meals is the main way we open ourselves to receive Christ in one another. Christ left us a meal as the memorial of his love. When we share meals, we celebrate love in Christ, and recall the sacred meal of the Eucharist.
- Invite feedback and general conversation about this illustration and its commentary (about five minutes).

Break

Pages four and five

The illustration

- Show the illustration on slide 5, which is the same as the one in the booklet. Invite the participants to look at the illustration. Ask questions such as: What does this image remind you of in your own life? What is the significance of the water?
- Refer to the quote on the back cover. "Jesus' public life begins with his baptism." Jesus' baptism reminds us that in baptism we are initiated into Christ. Baptism calls us to conversion. As part of the Christian mystery, in order to rise with Christ, we must first repent and die to ourselves in Christ.
- Invite feedback on this illustration and its commentary (about 5 minutes).

Read and reflect

- Ask participants to read pages four and five. Follow the same process for reading and reflection that you used for the first pages.

Share it with others

- Read the reflection on slide 6 and/or the reflection(s) provided in the booklet. Use the same format for group discussion and sharing as you did for the previous pages.
- Use PowerPoint slide 7 to provide the group with a visual of a Scripture passage. Open your Bibles to Luke 3:4, and select a few verses to read aloud. How does this Scripture passage relate to what you have just read and discussed?
- Pause for a few moments of silence.

Pages six and seven

Personal experience

- Ask everyone to look at the heading on page six, "Message." Invite them to reflect on these questions: What kind of messages do I receive every day? Where and from whom? Which do I consider to be the most important? Do I listen to the message of Christ daily?

Read and reflect

- Again, follow the same process for reading and reflection on pages six and seven.

Share it with others

- Read the reflection on slide 8 and/or the reflection(s) provided in the booklet. Use the same format for group discussion and sharing.

- Use PowerPoint slide 9 to provide the group with a visual of a Scripture passage. Open your Bibles to Matthew 16:18, and select a few verses to read aloud. How does this Scripture passage relate to what you have just read and discussed?

- Pause for a few moments of silence, then ask the participants to look at the illustration on slide 10, which is the same as the one on these pages. Refer to the quote on the back cover. Christ chose one disciple to become the shepherd of his flock. In this act, he established the way we Christians would be organized ever since. "From the beginning of his public life Jesus chose certain men to be with him and to participate in his mission.... Peter holds the first place in the college of the Twelve.... Because of the faith [Peter] confessed, he will remain the unshakable rock of the Church" (*Catechism*, 551–552). The keys of St. Peter are a symbol of his authority.

Exercise

- Invite the participants to choose two symbols of Christ's life and do a drawing of each. Ask them to share what significance the symbols have for them. This activity can help them think more about what Christ's life means for them.

Take it home

- Before the end of the evening, ask the small groups to talk once more about how they plan to take home and live what they have learned. Refer to the reflections, and suggest they use them to help apply the core message of this booklet. Invite them to make concrete and realistic plans. Allow a few minutes for this discussion.

Conclusion

- Go to slide 11 and announce the time and place of the next gathering.

- Go to slide 12 and invite everyone to pray the closing prayer aloud. (You can make copies of the prayer, found on page 29 of this guide, or use the prayer of Blessed John XXIII on page 5.) You can, instead, invite the group to offer spontaneous prayer. You may also close the evening with the dismissal song on the CD.

Session Plan for Reflection Booklet **14**

Why Did Jesus Suffer?

Content summary

The passion of Christ (based on articles 557–570 and 595–623 in the *Catechism of the Catholic Church*)

- Jesus' prophetic voice threatened the church leaders of his day.
- The Jews are not responsible for the death of Christ.
- Jesus gave us a tremendous sign of his love at the Last Supper when he washed the feet of his disciples.
- Jesus freely offered himself for our salvation.

Preparation

- Read through the booklet once, reflectively. Reread it and make your own notes.
- Read through the session plan and become comfortable with the format.
- For more background, read articles 557–570 and 595–623 of the *Catechism*. Mark and look up any unfamiliar words.
- Decide if and when you will do the exercise found after the material for pages six and seven. Have the materials needed.
- See pages 12–13 in this guide for other steps for preparation and materials needed.

Opening

- After introductions, if the number of participants is ten or more, ask them to form small groups. If the assembly is a large one, have each group choose a spokesperson.
- Have PowerPoint slide 1 (the cover illustration) on the screen as you begin.
- Open with the prayer found on page 4 in the introductory section of this guide. You may make copies for the participants. Or use the gathering song on the CD.
- Use the Question of the Week approach to break open the word of God from the Sunday liturgy (see 6 on page 12). Then continue with the *Growing Faith* booklet.

Pages two and three

Read and reflect

- Make sure everyone has a copy of the booklet.
- Ask the participants to read pages two and three of the booklet quietly. Tell them they will have a few minutes to do so (about five minutes).
- Invite them to mark the text when they read something that strikes them.

Share it with others

- Read the reflection on slide 2 and/or the reflection(s) provided in the booklet. Ask participants to discuss these questions in their small groups as a means of applying what they have learned in the text. Encourage them to take notes in their booklets. Give them several minutes to do all this. You may wish to play quiet music in the background during this time.
- If the assembly is large, ask the spokesperson of each small group to share a summary of the group's discussion with the larger group. Write on the board a short version or outline of all the responses.
- Use the PowerPoint slide 3 to provide the group with a visual of a Scripture passage. Open your Bibles to Matthew 25:34, 36, and select a few verses to read aloud. How does this Scripture passage relate to what you have just read and discussed?
- Pause for a few moments of silence, then go to the illustration on slide 4, which is also found in the booklet. Ask the participants to look at the illustration. On the back cover you will find a reference for this illustration, from Scripture or the *Catechism*, that may assist you. When we serve one another with kindness and caring, we share in Christ's own loving service to us. We die to our selfishness and self-centeredness on behalf of others, and find our true fulfillment. "Because in his incarnate divine person Christ has in some way united himself to every [person], 'the possibility of being made partners…in the paschal mystery' is offered to all [of us]" (*Catechism*, 618).
- Invite feedback and general conversation about this illustration and its commentary (about five minutes).

Break

Pages four and five

The illustration

- Show the illustration on slide 5, which is the same as the one in the booklet. Invite the participants to look at the illustration. Ask questions such as: Is the cross a negative or a positive icon for you? Why?
- These different crosses come from various cultures and even various rites in the church. Design your own cross.
- Refer to the quote on the back cover. "The cross is the unique sacrifice of Christ." For us Christians, the cross—in whatever shape we honor it—is a symbol of the paschal mystery of Christ. It is also a reminder of Christ's love for us.
- Invite feedback on this illustration and its commentary (about 5 minutes).

Read and reflect

- Ask participants to read pages four and five. Follow the same process for reading and reflection that you used for the first pages.

Share it with others

- Read the reflection on slide 6 and/or the reflection(s) provided in the booklet. Use the same format for group discussion and sharing as you did for the previous pages.
- Use PowerPoint slide 7 to provide the group with a visual of a Scripture passage. Open your Bibles to 1 John 4:9, and select a few verses to read aloud. How does this Scripture passage relate to what you have just read and discussed?
- Pause for a few moments of silence.

Pages six and seven

Personal experience

- Ask everyone to look at the heading on page seven, "The garden." Invite them to reflect on these questions: What images does the word "garden" bring to mind? What did "garden" mean for Jesus?

Read and reflect

- Again, follow the same process for reading and reflection on pages six and seven.

Share it with others

- Read the reflection on slide 8 and/or the reflection(s) provided in the booklet. Use the same format for group discussion and sharing.
- Use PowerPoint slide 9 to provide the group with a visual of a Scripture passage. Open your Bibles to Matthew 16:24, and select a few verses to read aloud. How does this Scripture passage relate to what you have just read and discussed?
- Pause for a few moments of silence, then go to slide 10. Ask the participants to look at the illustration, which is the same as the one on these pages. Refer to the quote on the back cover. Christ's mission [was] to "serve and give his life." Mother Teresa is an example of someone who has responded to Christ's invitation to serve and love each other. As Christ gave his life in sacrifice, so we may make small sacrifices to show our love. How can we imitate Mother Teresa's example of love in our own lives?

Exercise

- Provide a copy of either an article or an entire newspaper for each person. Then invite them to do the exercise on page four of the booklet, which asks them to read one or more major articles from the perspective of faith. Can they find anything in the articles that reflects Christian values in practice, or in the way the article is written?

Take it home

- Before the end of the evening, ask the small groups to talk once more about how they plan to take home and live what they have learned. Refer to the reflections, and suggest they use them to help apply the core message of this booklet. Invite them to make concrete and realistic plans. Allow a few minutes for this discussion.

Conclusion

- Go to slide 11 and announce the time and place of the next gathering.
- Go to slide 12 and invite everyone to pray the closing prayer aloud. (You can make copies of the prayer, found on page 29 of this guide, or use the prayer of Blessed John XXIII on page 5.) You can, instead, invite the group to offer spontaneous prayer. You may also close the evening with the dismissal song on the CD..

Session Plan for Reflection Booklet **15**

Why Do You Look for the Living Among the Dead?

Content summary

The Resurrection and the Ascension (based on articles 624–682 in the *Catechism of the Catholic Church*)

- The early followers of Christ experienced him alive among them after his death.
- They especially felt his presence while sharing meals.
- In baptism we enter into the death of the Lord, so we can also enter into his resurrection.
- Christ now lives with God from whom he came. He opens for us the way to eternal life with God.

Preparation

- Read through the booklet once, reflectively. Reread it and make your own notes.
- Read through the session plan and become comfortable with the format.
- For more background, read articles 624–682 of the *Catechism*. Mark and look up any unfamiliar words.
- Decide if and when you will do the exercise found after the material for pages six and seven. Have the materials needed.
- See pages 12–13 in this guide for other steps for preparation and materials needed.

Opening

- After introductions, if the number of participants is ten or more, ask them to form small groups. If the assembly is a large one, have each group choose a spokesperson.
- Have PowerPoint slide 1 (the cover illustration) on the screen as you begin.
- Open with the prayer found on page 4 in the introductory section of this guide. You may make copies for the participants. Or use the gathering song on the CD.
- Use the Question of the Week approach to break open the word of God from the Sunday liturgy (see 6 on page 12). Then continue with the *Growing Faith* booklet.

Pages two and three

Read and reflect

- Make sure everyone has a copy of the booklet.
- Ask the participants to read pages two and three of the booklet quietly. Tell them they will have a few minutes to do so (about five minutes).
- Invite them to mark the text when they read something that strikes them.

Share it with others

- Read the reflection on slide 2 and/or the reflection(s) provided in the booklet. Ask participants to discuss these questions in their small groups as a means of applying what they have learned in the text. Encourage them to take notes in their booklets. Give them several minutes to do all this. You may wish to play quiet music in the background during this time.
- If the assembly is large, ask the spokesperson of each small group to share a summary of the group's discussion with the larger group. Write on the board a short version or outline of all the responses.
- Use the PowerPoint slide 3 to provide the group with a visual of a Scripture passage. Open your Bibles to Mark 16:6, and select a few verses to read aloud. How does this Scripture passage relate to what you have just read and discussed?
- Pause for a few moments of silence, then go to the illustration on slide 4, which is also found in the booklet. Ask the participants to look at the illustration. On the back cover you will find a reference for this illustration, from Scripture or the *Catechism*, that may assist you. We often think of Easter as a time when lilies bloom, and how appropriate that is. Resurrection is like the blossom of new life, a the opening of new life, a fresh beginning. "It is the God who said, 'Let light shine out of darkness,' who has shone in our hearts to give the light of the knowledge of the glory of God in the face of Jesus Christ…. We know that the one who raised the Lord Jesus will raise us also with Jesus, and will bring us with you into his presence" (2 Corinthians 4:6, 14).
- Invite feedback and general conversation about this illustration and its commentary (about five minutes).

Break

Pages four and five

The illustration

- Show the illustration on slide 5, which is the same as the one in the booklet. Invite the participants to look at the illustration. Ask questions such as: Have you heard the word "agape" before? It's a Greek word that means "sacred love." How and when would you apply that word to your life?
- Refer to the quote on the back cover. "The disciples broke bread at home and ate their food with glad and generous hearts." For the early Christians, shared supper meals were sacred. They were called "love feasts," which is another meaning of "agape." They recalled the meals Jesus shared with his followers.
- Invite feedback on this illustration and its commentary (about 5 minutes).

Read and reflect

- Ask participants to read pages four and five. Follow the same process for reading and reflection that you used for the first pages.

Share it with others

- Read the reflection on slide 6 and/or the reflection(s) provided in the booklet. Use the same format for group discussion and sharing as you did for the previous pages.
- Use PowerPoint slide 7 to provide the group with a visual of a Scripture passage. Open your Bibles to Luke 24:30–31, and select a few verses to read aloud. How does this Scripture passage relate to what you have just read and discussed?
- Pause for a few moments of silence.

Pages six and seven

Personal experience

- Ask everyone to look at the heading on page six, "He is ascended!" Invite them to reflect on these questions: What comes to mind when I read these words? What does "ascended" mean to me? Do the words have any impact on my daily life now? Why or why not?

Read and reflect

- Again, follow the same process for reading and reflection on pages six and seven.

Share it with others

- Read the reflection on slide 8 and/or the reflection(s) provided in the booklet. Use the same format for group discussion and sharing.

- Use PowerPoint slide 9 to provide the group with a visual of a Scripture passage. Open your Bibles to John 21:9, 12, and select a few verses to read aloud. How does this Scripture passage relate to what you have just read and discussed?

- Pause for a few moments of silence, then ask the participants to look at the illustration on slide 10, which is the same as the one on these pages. Refer to the quote on the back cover. After his resurrection Jesus appeared to his followers almost always in the context of a meal. This illustration depicts the famous "fish fry" on the beach described in the Gospel of John. On another occasion Jesus walked with the disciples on their way to Emmaus. These two people did not recognize him until they began their meal, during which Jesus blessed and broke the bread. "Then their eyes were opened" (Luke 24:13–35). We, also, experience the risen Lord in the context of meals. He is present, not absent in the church.

Exercise

- Provide a large piece of felt for each group, plus other materials for making a banner. Ask each group to choose one of the large quotes from pages two to five and make a banner with that quote (e.g., "Jesus Christ tasted death for the benefit of all"). Hang the banners in your parish church.

Take it home

- Before the end of the evening, ask the small groups to talk once more about how they plan to take home and live what they have learned. Refer to the reflections, and suggest they use them to help apply the core message of this booklet. Invite them to make concrete and realistic plans. Allow a few minutes for this discussion.

Conclusion

- Go to slide 11 and announce the time and place of the next gathering.

- Go to slide 12 and invite everyone to pray the closing prayer aloud. (You can make copies of the prayer, found on page 29 of this guide, or use the prayer of Blessed John XXIII on page 5.) You can, instead, invite the group to offer spontaneous prayer. You may also close the evening with the dismissal song on the CD.

Session Plan for Reflection Booklet **16**

Who Guides and Inspires You?

Content summary

The Holy Spirit (based on articles 683–747 in the *Catechism of the Catholic Church*)

- Whenever God sends Christ, he always sends the Spirit: their mission is one and inseparable.
- In the fullness of time the Holy Spirit completed in Mary all the preparations for Christ's coming among the people of God.
- The Holy Spirit, whom Christ sends, builds, animates, and sanctifies the church.
- The church is the sacrament of the Holy Trinity's communion with us.

Preparation

- Read through the booklet once, reflectively. Reread it and make your own notes.
- Read through the session plan and become comfortable with the format.
- For more background, read articles 683–747 of the *Catechism*. Mark and look up any unfamiliar words.
- Decide if and when you will do the exercise found after the material for pages six and seven. Have the materials needed.
- See pages 12–13 in this guide for other steps for preparation and materials needed.

Opening

- After introductions, if the number of participants is ten or more, ask them to form small groups. If the assembly is a large one, have each group choose a spokesperson.
- Have PowerPoint slide 1 (the cover illustration) on the screen as you begin.
- Open with the prayer found on page 4 in the introductory section of this guide. You may make copies for the participants. Or use the gathering song on the CD.
- Use the Question of the Week approach to break open the word of God from the Sunday liturgy (see 6 on page 12). Then continue with the *Growing Faith* booklet.

Pages two and three

Read and reflect

- Make sure everyone has a copy of the booklet.
- Ask the participants to read pages two and three of the booklet quietly. Tell them they will have a few minutes to do so (about five minutes).
- Invite them to mark the text when they read something that strikes them.

Share it with others

- Read the reflection on slide 2 and/or the reflection(s) provided in the booklet. Ask participants to discuss these questions in their small groups as a means of applying what they have learned in the text. Encourage them to take notes in their booklets. Give them several minutes to do all this. You may wish to play quiet music in the background during this time.
- If the assembly is large, ask the spokesperson of each small group to share a summary of the group's discussion with the larger group. Write on the board a short version or outline of all the responses.
- Use the PowerPoint slide 3 to provide the group with a visual of a Scripture passage. Open your Bibles to 1 Corinthians 12:3b, and select a few verses to read aloud. How does this Scripture passage relate to what you have just read and discussed?
- Pause for a few moments of silence, then go to the illustration on slide 4, which is also found in the booklet. Ask the participants to look at the illustration. On the back cover you will find a reference for this illustration, from Scripture or the *Catechism*, that may assist you. When the Spirit is with us, we are empowered and enlightened. This experience is often described as a fire burning within us. As in the picture with the girl holding the candle, "fire symbolizes the transforming energy of the Holy Spirit's actions" (*Catechism*, 696). In fact, on Pentecost the Holy Spirit came to the disciples in the form of tongues "as of fire."
- Invite feedback and general conversation about this illustration and its commentary (about five minutes).

Break

Pages four and five

The illustration

- Show the illustration on slide 5, which is the same as the one in the booklet. Invite the participants to look at the illustration. Ask questions such as: What do you see in this image? What meaning does it have for you? What does "blessing" mean to you?
- Refer to the quote on the back cover. "Jesus heals the sick and blesses the little children." As Christians we often lay hands on or over another person's head as a way of invoking a blessing. Blessing one another in this way is a lovely way for us to share God's love within our community. It is a sign of the Holy Spirit, and the Spirit's action in our lives.
- Invite feedback on this illustration and its commentary (about 5 minutes).

Read and reflect

- Ask participants to read pages four and five. Follow the same process for reading and reflection that you used for the first pages.

Share it with others

- Read the reflection on slide 6 and/or the reflection(s) provided in the booklet. Use the same format for group discussion and sharing as you did for the previous pages.
- Use PowerPoint slide 7 to provide the group with a visual of a Scripture passage. Open your Bibles to Mark 10:16, and select a few verses to read aloud. How does this Scripture passage relate to what you have just read and discussed?
- Pause for a few moments of silence.

Pages six and seven

Personal experience

- Ask everyone to look at the heading on page six, "The Spirit in the New Testament." Invite them to reflect on these questions: When I read or hear about the Holy Spirit in the gospels, in Acts of the Apostles, or in the letters, does what I read have any bearing on my life? When have I experienced the movement or action of the Spirit in my heart, e.g., in prayer, in the desire to do good, in a longing for God?
- Invite everyone to draw their own symbol for the Spirit.

Read and reflect

- Again, follow the same process for reading and reflection on pages six and seven.

Share it with others

- Read the reflection on slide 8 and/or the reflection(s) provided in the booklet. Use the same format for group discussion and sharing.
- Use PowerPoint slide 9 to provide the group with a visual of a Scripture passage. Open your Bibles to Acts 2:2, and select a few verses to read aloud. How does this Scripture passage relate to what you have just read and discussed?
- Pause for a few moments of silence, then ask the participants to look at the illustration on slide 10, which is the same as the one on these pages. Refer to the quote on the back cover. The Spirit of God "blows where it wills," which means we must be ready at any moment to be moved by the Spirit. Like these curtains blowing in the wind, we must be supple and flexible so we can respond when the opportunity to serve or love presents itself. Such occasions appear in our lives every day. The gifts of the Holy Spirit make us more sensitive to and aware of the Spirit's action within us, more open to the practice of the virtues.

Exercise

- Ask the participants to reread the last paragraph on page five, a description of the gifts of the Holy Spirit. Ask them to write down some concrete ways in which these gifts help them in their daily lives.

Take it home

- Before the end of the evening, ask the small groups to talk once more about how they plan to take home and live what they have learned. Refer to the reflections, and suggest they use them to help apply the core message of this booklet. Invite them to make concrete and realistic plans. Allow a few minutes for this discussion.

Conclusion

- Go to slide 11 and announce the time and place of the next gathering.
- Go to slide 12 and invite everyone to pray the closing prayer aloud. (You can make copies of the prayer, found on page 29 of this guide, or use the prayer of Blessed John XXIII on page 5.) You can, instead, invite the group to offer spontaneous prayer. You may also close the evening with the dismissal song on the CD.

Session Plan for Reflection Booklet **17**

With Whom Do You Gather?

Content summary

The mystery of the church (based on articles 748–810 in the *Catechism of the Catholic Church*)

- The word "church" designates the assembly of those whom God's word convokes, i.e. gathers together to form the people of God. They are nourished with the body of Christ, become the body of Christ.
- The church in this world is the sacrament of salvation, the sign and instrument of God's communion with us.
- We become members of the people of God through faith and baptism.
- The church is the body of Christ, the bride of Christ, and the temple of the Holy Spirit.

Preparation

- Read through the booklet once, reflectively. Reread it and make your own notes.
- Read through the session plan and become comfortable with the format.
- For more background, read articles 748–810 of the *Catechism*. Mark and look up any unfamiliar words.
- Decide if and when you will do the exercise found after the material for pages six and seven. Have the materials needed.
- See pages 12–13 in this guide for other steps for preparation and materials needed.

Opening

- After introductions, if the number of participants is ten or more, ask them to form small groups. If the assembly is a large one, have each group choose a spokesperson.
- Have PowerPoint slide 1 (the cover illustration) on the screen as you begin.
- Open with the prayer found on page 4 in the introductory section of this guide. You may make copies for the participants. Or use the gathering song on the CD.
- Use the Question of the Week approach to break open the word of God from the Sunday liturgy (see 6 on page 12). Then continue with the *Growing Faith* booklet.

Pages two and three

Read and reflect

- Make sure everyone has a copy of the booklet.
- Ask the participants to read pages two and three of the booklet quietly. Tell them they will have a few minutes to do so (about five minutes).
- Invite them to mark the text when they read something that strikes them.

Share it with others

- Read the reflection on slide 2 and/or the reflection(s) provided in the booklet. Ask participants to discuss these questions in their small groups as a means of applying what they have learned in the text. Encourage them to take notes in their booklets. Give them several minutes to do all this. You may wish to play quiet music in the background during this time.
- If the assembly is large, ask the spokesperson of each small group to share a summary of the group's discussion with the larger group. Write on the board a short version or outline of all the responses.
- Use the PowerPoint slide 3 to provide the group with a visual of a Scripture passage. Open your Bibles to Ephesians 1:9, and select a few verses to read aloud. How does this Scripture passage relate to what you have just read and discussed?
- Pause for a few moments of silence, then go to the illustration on slide 4, which is also found in the booklet. Ask the participants to look at the illustration. On the back cover you will find a reference for this illustration, from Scripture or the *Catechism*, that may assist you. The church building provides a place for us to celebrate together, but in fact we ourselves are the church. We can celebrate anywhere, at any time. One name for the church is "the building of God, the household of God, with Christ as the cornerstone." St. Paul speaks of the church as the temple, built of living stones. "In Christian usage, the word 'church' designates the liturgical assembly, but also the local community or the universal community of believers. These three meanings are inseparable.... [The Church] draws her life from the word and the Body of Christ and so herself becomes Christ's Body" (*Catechism* ,752).
- Invite feedback and general conversation about this illustration and its commentary (about five minutes).

Break

Pages four and five

The illustration

- Show the illustration on slide 5, which is the same as the one in the booklet. Invite the participants to look at the illustration. Ask questions such as: For a moment forget about the gospel image of the good shepherd. What does this picture say to you right at this moment? Is the image of a shepherd caring for a sheep meaningful for you? Why or why not? What other image would you choose?

- Refer to the quote on the back cover. "The Church is a sheepfold…. It is also the flock." Those who tend sheep must be very gentle and steady, as sheep are easily frightened. Shepherds keep careful watch over their flocks and come to care very much for their sheep. Jesus shows the same loving care for us. Reflection on Psalm 23 offers examples of the intimate love and care of God and the church that the shepherd symbolize.

- Invite feedback on this illustration and its commentary (about 5 minutes).

Read and reflect

- Ask participants to read pages four and five. Follow the same process for reading and reflection that you used for the first pages.

Share it with others

- Read the reflection on slide 6 and/or the reflection(s) provided in the booklet. Use the same format for group discussion and sharing as you did for the previous pages.

- Use PowerPoint slide 7 to provide the group with a visual of a Scripture passage. Open your Bibles to John 10:11, and select a few verses to read aloud. How does this Scripture passage relate to what you have just read and discussed?

- Pause for a few moments of silence.

Pages six and seven

Personal experience

- Ask everyone to look at the heading on page seven, "Temple of the Holy Spirit." Invite them to reflect on these questions: How would you describe a "temple"? What would its characteristics be? Have you thought of yourself as a temple of the Holy Spirit? Apart from theological reflections, what feelings and images does this comparison evoke in you?

Read and reflect

- Again, follow the same process for reading and reflection on pages six and seven.

Share it with others

- Read the reflection on slide 8 and/or the reflection(s) provided in the booklet. Use the same format for group discussion and sharing.
- Use PowerPoint slide 9 to provide the group with a visual of a Scripture passage. Open your Bibles to Colossians 2:6, and select a few verses to read aloud. How does this Scripture passage relate to what you have just read and discussed?
- Pause for a few moments of silence, then ask the participants to look at the illustration on slide 10, which is the same as the one on these pages. Refer to the quote on the back cover. Too often Catholics have been taught to be solemn and serious about and in our religion, and there are certainly times for that, too. But we have a lot to celebrate in our faith! God loves us while we are still sinners, and we are given love to share with others. Like these musicians, we make merry and dance because of this Good News!

Exercise

- Invite the participants to do the exercise on page seven, which asks them to think about the gifts the church needs to accomplish her mission. Completing this activity will raise a more profound awareness of ourselves and our calling as church.

Take it home

- Before the end of the evening, ask the small groups to talk once more about how they plan to take home and live what they have learned. Refer to the reflections, and suggest they use them to help apply the core message of this booklet. Invite them to make concrete and realistic plans. Allow a few minutes for this discussion.

Conclusion

- Go to slide 11 and announce the time and place of the next gathering.
- Go to slide 12 and invite everyone to pray the closing prayer aloud. (You can make copies of the prayer, found on page 29 of this guide, or use the prayer of Blessed John XXIII on page 5.) You can, instead, invite the group to offer spontaneous prayer. You may also close the evening with the dismissal song on the CD.

Session Plan for Reflection Booklet **18**

How Do You Recognize the Church?

Content summary

The Church is one, holy, Catholic, and apostolic (based on articles 811-870 in the *Catechism of the Catholic Church*)

- The Jewish faith is already a response to God's revelation in the Old Covenant. Neither Jews at that time nor Jews today can be blamed indiscriminately for the suffering Christ endured during his passion.
- Those who do not know the gospel of Christ or his church may yet seek God with a sincere heart. Moved by grace, they try to do God's will as they know it through the dictates of their conscience. These persons, also, may achieve eternal salvation.
- The Holy Spirit is the "principal agent of the whole of the Church's mission." As the mission of the church continues, it fulfills the mission of Christ.

Preparation

- Read through the booklet once, reflectively. Reread it and make your own notes.
- Read through the session plan and become comfortable with the format.
- For more background, read articles 811–870 of the *Catechism*. Mark and look up any unfamiliar words.
- Decide if and when you will do the exercise found after the material for pages six and seven. Have the materials needed.
- See pages 12–13 in this guide for other steps for preparation and materials needed.

Opening

- After introductions, if the number of participants is ten or more, ask them to form small groups. If the assembly is a large one, have each group choose a spokesperson.
- Have PowerPoint slide 1 (the cover illustration) on the screen as you begin.
- Open with the prayer found on page 4 in the introductory section of this guide. You may make copies for the participants. Or use the gathering song on the CD.
- Use the Question of the Week approach to break open the word of God from the Sunday liturgy (see 6 on page 12). Then continue with the *Growing Faith* booklet.

Pages two and three

Read and reflect

- Make sure everyone has a copy of the booklet.
- Ask the participants to read pages two and three of the booklet quietly. Tell them they will have a few minutes to do so (about five minutes).
- Invite them to mark the text when they read something that strikes them.

Share it with others

- Read the reflection on slide 2 and/or the reflection(s) provided in the booklet. Ask participants to discuss these questions in their small groups as a means of applying what they have learned in the text. Encourage them to take notes in their booklets. Give them several minutes to do all this. You may wish to play quiet music in the background during this time.
- If the assembly is large, ask the spokesperson of each small group to share a summary of the group's discussion with the larger group. Write on the board a short version or outline of all the responses.
- Use the PowerPoint slide 3 to provide the group with a visual of a Scripture passage. Open your Bibles to Ephesians 4:4–5, and select a few verses to read aloud. How does this Scripture passage relate to what you have just read and discussed?
- Pause for a few moments of silence, then go to the illustration on slide 4, which is also found in the booklet. Ask the participants to look at the illustration. On the back cover you will find a reference for this illustration, from Scripture or the *Catechism*, that may assist you. St. Paul was an apostle filled with love for Christ and his sisters and brothers. He proclaimed the gospel whenever and wherever possible. In his journeys he encouraged and established Christian communities. "The gifts he gave were…to equip the saints for the world of ministry, for building up the body of Christ, until all of us come to the unity of the faiths" (Ephesians 4:11–13).
- Invite feedback and general conversation about this illustration and its commentary (about five minutes).

Break

Pages four and five

The illustration

- Show the illustration on slide 5, which is the same as the one in the booklet. Invite the participants to look at the illustration. Ask questions such as: What do you see in this image? Who do you think these people might be? Their backgrounds, their concerns, their desires? Can you relate to these?
- Refer to the quote on the back cover. "The Church strives to preach the Gospel to all [people]." The church has always had missionaries, persons called to bring the Good News to people around the world. The church is present in all local parishes, united by communion with the church of Rome.
- Invite feedback on this illustration and its commentary (about 5 minutes).

Read and reflect

- Ask participants to read pages four and five. Follow the same process for reading and reflection that you used for the first pages.

Share it with others

- Read the reflection on slide 6 and/or the reflection(s) provided in the booklet. Use the same format for group discussion and sharing as you did for the previous pages.
- Use PowerPoint slide 7 to provide the group with a visual of a Scripture passage. Open your Bibles to Matthew 5:13–14, and select a few verses to read aloud. How does this Scripture passage relate to what you have just read and discussed?
- Pause for a few moments of silence.

Pages six and seven

Personal experience

- Ask everyone to look at the heading on page six, "Tell it on the mountain." Invite them to reflect on these questions: What does this expression, which is also part of an old spiritual, mean to you? When, where, and how have you proclaimed the gospel, even in small ways, in your own family, at work, in your neighborhood, and so on?

Read and reflect

- Again, follow the same process for reading and reflection on pages six and seven.

Share it with others

- Read the reflection on slide 8 and/or the reflection(s) provided in the booklet. Use the same format for group discussion and sharing.
- Use PowerPoint slide 9 to provide the group with a visual of a Scripture passage. Open your Bibles to John 17:20, 21a, and select a few verses to read aloud. How does this Scripture passage relate to what you have just read and discussed?
- Pause for a few moments of silence, then ask the participants to look at the illustration on slide 10, which is the same as the one on these pages. Refer to the quote on the back cover. The church is the people of God assembled, as shown here, for the Eucharist. Whenever we gather, Christ is among us, inviting us to be more united with each other, more holy, more universal in our view of mission, and more connected to the faith of the early church, which is the apostolic faith.

Exercise

- Invite the participants to write their own prayers for the church.

Take it home

- Before the end of the evening, ask the small groups to talk once more about how they plan to take home and live what they have learned. Refer to the reflections, and suggest they use them to help apply the core message of this booklet. Invite them to make concrete and realistic plans. Allow a few minutes for this discussion.

Conclusion

- Go to slide 11 and announce the time and place of the next gathering.
- Go to slide 12 and invite everyone to pray the closing prayer aloud. (You can make copies of the prayer, found on page 29 of this guide, or use the prayer of Blessed John XXIII on page 5.) You can, instead, invite the group to offer spontaneous prayer. You may also close the evening with the dismissal song on the CD.

Session Plan for Reflection Booklet **19**

Who Is the Church?

Content summary

Christ's faithful: the people of the church (based on articles 871–945 in the *Catechism of the Catholic Church*)

- To proclaim the faith and establish his reign, Christ sends his apostles and their successors. He gives them a share in his own mission. From him they receive the power to act in his person.
- The bishop of the church of Rome, successor to St. Peter, is "head of the college of bishops, the Vicar of Christ and Pastor of the universal Church on earth."
- Helped by the priests, by their coworkers, and by the deacons, the bishops have the duty of authentically teaching the faith, celebrating divine worship, above all the Eucharist, and guiding their churches as true pastors.
- As lay people we share in Christ's priesthood. United with him, we live out the grace of baptism and confirmation in all dimensions of our personal, family, social, and ecclesial lives. In this way we fulfill the call to holiness addressed to all baptized persons.

Preparation

- Read through the booklet once, reflectively. Reread it and make your own notes.
- Read through the session plan and become comfortable with the format.
- For more background, read articles 871–945 of the *Catechism*. Mark and look up any unfamiliar words.
- Decide if and when you will do the exercise found after the material for pages six and seven. Have the materials needed.
- See pages 12–13 in this guide for other steps for preparation and materials needed.

Opening

- After introductions, if the number of participants is ten or more, ask them to form small groups. If the assembly is a large one, have each group choose a spokesperson.
- Have PowerPoint slide 1 (the cover illustration) on the screen as you begin.

- Open with the prayer found on page 4 in the introductory section of this guide. You may make copies for the participants. Or use the gathering song on the CD.
- Use the Question of the Week approach to break open the word of God from the Sunday liturgy (see 6 on page 12). Then continue with the *Growing Faith* booklet.

Pages two and three

Read and reflect

- Make sure everyone has a copy of the booklet.
- Ask the participants to read pages two and three of the booklet quietly. Tell them they will have a few minutes to do so (about five minutes).
- Invite them to mark the text when they read something that strikes them.

Share it with others

- Read the reflection on slide 2 and/or the reflection(s) provided in the booklet. Ask participants to discuss these questions in their small groups as a means of applying what they have learned in the text. Encourage them to take notes in their booklets. Give them several minutes to do all this. You may wish to play quiet music in the background during this time.
- If the assembly is large, ask the spokesperson of each small group to share a summary of the group's discussion with the larger group. Write on the board a short version or outline of all the responses.
- Use the PowerPoint slide 3 to provide the group with a visual of a Scripture passage. Open your Bibles to 1 Peter 5:3, and select a few verses to read aloud. How does this Scripture passage relate to what you have just read and discussed?
- Pause for a few moments of silence, then go to the illustration on slide 4, which is also found in the booklet. Ask the participants to look at the illustration. On the back cover you will find a reference for this illustration, from Scripture or the *Catechism*, that may assist you. Explain that bishops are called to work among the people of God as servants, assisting them in their journey of faith. In this way the church is organized from the pope and bishops upward (or outward) to the people of God.
- Invite feedback and general conversation about this illustration and its commentary (about five minutes).

Break

Pages four and five

The illustration

- Show the illustration on slide 5, which is the same as the one in the booklet. Invite the participants to look at the illustration. Ask questions such as: What do you know about the role of the pope? How does his role affect your life as a Catholic Christian?
- Refer to the quote on the back cover. "The Lord made Simon…the 'rock' of his church." The pope is a sign of unity for Catholics worldwide. We all draw strength from being part of the same flock with the same shepherd. "In order to shepherd the People of God and to increase its numbers without cease, Christ the Lord set up in his Church a variety of offices which aim at the good of the whole body. The holders of office, who are invested with a sacred power, are in fact dedicated to promoting the interests of their [brothers and sisters]" (*Catechism*, 874).
- Invite feedback on this illustration and its commentary (about 5 minutes).

Read and reflect

- Ask participants to read pages four and five. Follow the same process for reading and reflection that you used for the first pages.

Share it with others

- Read the reflection on slide 6 and/or the reflection(s) provided in the booklet. Use the same format for group discussion and sharing as you did for the previous pages.
- Use PowerPoint slide 7 to provide the group with a visual of a Scripture passage. Open your Bibles to 1 Peter 2:9, and select a few verses to read aloud. How does this Scripture passage relate to what you have just read and discussed?
- Pause for a few moments of silence.

Pages six and seven

Personal experience

- Ask everyone to look at the second heading on page six, "Religious life." Invite them to reflect on these questions: What is "religious life"? What do I know about the life of men and women religious? How do they impact my life?

Read and reflect

- Again, follow the same process for reading and reflection on pages six and seven.

Share it with others

- Read the reflection on slide 8 and/or the reflection(s) provided in the booklet. Use the same format for group discussion and sharing.
- Use PowerPoint slide 9 to provide the group with a visual of a Scripture passage. Open your Bibles to 1 Peter 2:5, and select a few verses to read aloud. How does this Scripture passage relate to what you have just read and discussed?
- Pause for a few moments of silence, then ask the participants to look at the illustration on slide 10, which is the same as the one on these pages. Refer to the quote on the back cover. When we speak of the faithful of the church, we include everyone: laity and religious, clergy, and even the catechumens. We are the church. We are God's holy and priestly people.

Exercise

- Invite the small groups to complete the "job descriptions" proposed in the exercise on page seven. This exercise should be informal, and the members can use whatever medium they choose (drawing, writing, and so on). This can function as a kind of review of the booklet's contents.

Take it home

- Before the end of the evening, ask the small groups to talk once more about how they plan to take home and live what they have learned. Refer to the reflections, and suggest they use them to help apply the core message of this booklet. Invite them to make concrete and realistic plans. Allow a few minutes for this discussion.

Conclusion

- Go to slide 11 and announce the time and place of the next gathering.
- Go to slide 12 and invite everyone to pray the closing prayer aloud. (You can make copies of the prayer, found on page 29 of this guide, or use the prayer of Blessed John XXIII on page 5.) You can, instead, invite the group to offer spontaneous prayer. You may also close the evening with the dismissal song on the CD.

Session Plan for Reflection Booklet **20**

What Happens at the End of Life?

Content summary

Heaven, purgatory, and hell (based on articles 946–962 and 976–1065 in the *Catechism of the Catholic Church*)

- The church is a "communion of saints," united above all by the Eucharist.
- After death we all receive our eternal recompense in a particular judgment by Christ.
- By virtue of the "communion of saints," the Church commends the dead to God's mercy and offers her prayers on their behalf, especially in the holy sacrifice of the Eucharist.
- Following the example of Christ, the church warns us of the "sad and lamentable reality of eternal death," also called "hell."

Preparation

- Read through the booklet once, reflectively. Reread it and make your own notes.
- Read through the session plan and become comfortable with the format.
- For more background, read articles 946–962 and 976–1065 of the *Catechism*. Mark and look up any unfamiliar words.
- Decide if and when you will do the exercise found after the material for pages six and seven. Have the materials needed.
- See pages 12–13 in this guide for other steps for preparation and materials needed.

Opening

- After introductions, if the number of participants is ten or more, ask them to form small groups. If the assembly is a large one, have each group choose a spokesperson.
- Have PowerPoint slide 1 (the cover illustration) on the screen as you begin.
- Open with the prayer found on page 4 in the introductory section of this guide. You may make copies for the participants. Or use the gathering song on the CD.
- Use the Question of the Week approach to break open the word of God from the Sunday liturgy (see 6 on page 12). Then continue with the *Growing Faith* booklet.

Pages two and three

Read and reflect

- Make sure everyone has a copy of the booklet.
- Ask the participants to read pages two and three of the booklet quietly. Tell them they will have a few minutes to do so (about five minutes).
- Invite them to mark the text when they read something that strikes them.

Share it with others

- Read the reflection on slide 2 and/or the reflection(s) provided in the booklet. Ask participants to discuss these questions in their small groups as a means of applying what they have learned in the text. Encourage them to take notes in their booklets. Give them several minutes to do all this. You may wish to play quiet music in the background during this time.
- If the assembly is large, ask the spokesperson of each small group to share a summary of the group's discussion with the larger group. Write on the board a short version or outline of all the responses.
- Use the PowerPoint slide 3 to provide the group with a visual of a Scripture passage. Open your Bibles to 1 Peter 3:8, and select a few verses to read aloud. How does this Scripture passage relate to what you have just read and discussed?
- Pause for a few moments of silence, then go to the illustration on slide 4, which is also found in the booklet. Ask the participants to look at the illustration. On the back cover you will find a reference for this illustration, from Scripture or the *Catechism*, that may assist you. Like this family all the faithful are part of the communion of saints. In fact, in the early church each baptized person was referred to as a saint. Through baptism we become part of this holy, all-encompassing family of God.
- Invite feedback and general conversation about this illustration and its commentary (about five minutes).

Break

Pages four and five

The illustration

- Show the illustration on slide 5, which is the same as the one in the booklet. Invite the participants to look at the illustration. Ask questions such as: What does this image of wheat signify to you? Why do you think only one wheat shaft has been broken? Can you recall any gospel passages referring to wheat?

- Refer to the quote on the back cover. "If [a grain of wheat] dies, it bears much fruit." As baptized persons we are called to give ourselves in love and service, dying to selfishness and self love, as Christ did. Like the grain of wheat, if we die we bear much fruit in eternal life. "Those who love their life lose it, and those who hate their life in this world will keep it for eternal life. Whoever serves me must follow me, and where I am, there will my servant be also" (John 12:25–26).

- Invite feedback on this illustration and its commentary (about 5 minutes).

Read and reflect

- Ask participants to read pages four and five. Follow the same process for reading and reflection that you used for the first pages.

Share it with others

- Read the reflection on slide 6 and/or the reflection(s) provided in the booklet. Use the same format for group discussion and sharing as you did for the previous pages.

- Use PowerPoint slide 7 to provide the group with a visual of a Scripture passage. Open your Bibles to Ecclesiastes 12:7, and select a few verses to read aloud. How does this Scripture passage relate to what you have just read and discussed?

- Pause for a few moments of silence.

Pages six and seven

Personal experience

- Ask everyone to look at the heading on page seven, "The last judgment." Invite them to reflect on these questions: What meaning does the word "judgment" have for me? What is my experience of human judgment? How do you think God's judgment will be different? How does thinking about the final judgment—and the personal judgment at the end of our lives—affect my daily choices?

Read and reflect

- Again, follow the same process for reading and reflection on pages six and seven.

Share it with others

- Read the reflection on slide 8 and/or the reflection(s) provided in the booklet. Use the same format for group discussion and sharing.
- Use PowerPoint slide 9 to provide the group with a visual of a Scripture passage. Open your Bibles to Matthew 16:26, and select a few verses to read aloud. How does this Scripture passage relate to what you have just read and discussed?
- Pause for a few moments of silence, then ask the participants to look at the illustration on slide 10, which is the same as the one on these pages. Refer to the quote on the back cover. Death is a part of life. The paradox is that we haven't really lived, as God means us to live, until we've died. Knowing we will die should shape the decisions we make in life, so we can enjoy the fullness of life in God.

Exercise

- Invite the participants in each small group to work together on the exercise proposed on page six, that is, to prepare a "litany of the saints."

Take it home

- Before the end of the evening, ask the small groups to talk once more about how they plan to take home and live what they have learned. Refer to the reflections, and suggest they use them to help apply the core message of this booklet. Invite them to make concrete and realistic plans. Allow a few minutes for this discussion.

Conclusion

- Go to slide 11 and announce the time and place of the next gathering.
- Go to slide 12 and invite everyone to pray the closing prayer aloud. (You can make copies of the prayer, found on page 29 of this guide, or use the prayer of Blessed John XXIII on page 5.) You can, instead, invite the group to offer spontaneous prayer. You may also close the evening with the dismissal song on the CD.

Session Plan for Reflection Booklet **21**

What Is the Liturgy?

Content summary

The liturgy is the work of the Trinity (based on articles 1066–1134 in the *Catechism of the Catholic Church*)

- In the liturgy of the church, God the Father is blessed as the source of all the gifts of creation. He has blessed us in Christ, so we might be God's adopted sons and daughters in the Spirit.
- Christ's work in the liturgy is sacramental. His body the church is a sacrament (sign and instrument) through which the Holy Spirit dispenses the mystery of salvation. Through her liturgical actions the pilgrim church already participates in the heavenly liturgy.
- The Holy Spirit prepares the assembly to encounter Christ in the liturgy.
- The sacraments are signs of grace, instituted by Christ and entrusted to the church. The celebration of their rites signifies and makes present the graces of each sacrament.

Preparation

- Read through the booklet once, reflectively. Reread it and make your own notes.
- Read through the session plan and become comfortable with the format.
- For more background, read articles 1066–1134 of the *Catechism*. Mark and look up any unfamiliar words.
- Decide if and when you will do the exercise found after the material for pages six and seven. Have the materials needed.
- See pages 12–13 in this guide for other steps for preparation and materials needed.

Opening

- After introductions, if the number of participants is ten or more, ask them to form small groups. If the assembly is a large one, have each group choose a spokesperson.
- Have PowerPoint slide 1 (the cover illustration) on the screen as you begin.
- Open with the prayer found on page 4 in the introductory section of this guide. You may make copies for the participants. Or use the gathering song on the CD.

- Use the Question of the Week approach to break open the word of God from the Sunday liturgy (see 6 on page 12). Then continue with the *Growing Faith* booklet.

Pages two and three

Read and reflect

- Make sure everyone has a copy of the booklet.
- Ask the participants to read pages two and three of the booklet quietly. Tell them they will have a few minutes to do so (about five minutes).
- Invite them to mark the text when they read something that strikes them.

Share it with others

- Read the reflection on slide 2 and/or the reflection(s) provided in the booklet. Ask participants to discuss these questions in their small groups as a means of applying what they have learned in the text. Encourage them to take notes in their booklets. Give them several minutes to do all this. You may wish to play quiet music in the background during this time.
- If the assembly is large, ask the spokesperson of each small group to share a summary of the group's discussion with the larger group. Write on the board a short version or outline of all the responses.
- Use the PowerPoint slide 3 to provide the group with a visual of a Scripture passage. Open your Bibles to Psalm 138, and select a few verses to read aloud. How does this Scripture passage relate to what you have just read and discussed?
- Pause for a few moments of silence, then go to the illustration on slide 4, which is also found in the booklet. Ask the participants to look at the illustration. On the back cover you will find a reference for this illustration, from Scripture or the *Catechism*, that may assist you. We gather together in church buildings for prayer, even though we know that we ourselves *are* the church wherever we happen to be! Still, the liturgy of the church is our lifehood. The Eucharist is the source and summit of the Christian life.
- Invite feedback and general conversation about this illustration and its commentary (about five minutes).

Break

Pages four and five

The illustration

- Show the illustration on slide 5, which is the same as the one in the booklet. Invite the participants to look at the illustration. Ask questions such as: Have you ever watched children praying? What are some special qualities of their prayer?

- Refer to the quote on the back cover. "The same marvelous work of God is internalized by all prayer." We are all called to pray with the innocence and trust of children. And we are called to grow in faith throughout our lives, embarking on a lifelong journey guided by the spirit who makes Christ present.

- Invite feedback on this illustration and its commentary (about 5 minutes).

Read and reflect

- Ask participants to read pages four and five. Follow the same process for reading and reflection that you used for the first pages.

Share it with others

- Read the reflection on slide 6 and/or the reflection(s) provided in the booklet. Use the same format for group discussion and sharing as you did for the previous pages.

- Use PowerPoint slide 7 to provide the group with a visual of a Scripture passage. Open your Bibles to Galatians 5:25, and select a few verses to read aloud. How does this Scripture passage relate to what you have just read and discussed?

- Pause for a few moments of silence.

Pages six and seven

Personal experience

- Ask everyone to look at the first heading on page seven, "In faith." Invite them to reflect on these questions: How strong or alive is my faith when I celebrate the sacraments? Has Sunday Eucharist become a repetition of actions and words, or the center of my spiritual growth?

Read and reflect

- Again, follow the same process for reading and reflection on pages six and seven.

Share it with others

- Read the reflection on slide 8 and/or the reflection(s) provided in the booklet. Use the same format for group discussion and sharing.
- Use PowerPoint slide 9 to provide the group with a visual of a Scripture passage. Open your Bibles to 1 Corinthians 12:27, and select a few verses to read aloud. How does this Scripture passage relate to what you have just read and discussed?
- Pause for a few moments of silence, then ask the participants to look at the illustration on slide 10, which is the same as the one on these pages. Refer to the quote on the back cover. When we turn our hearts to prayer, we invite God to dwell with us in a special and important way. The prayer of the community is the chief work of the church. "The word 'liturgy' originally meant a 'public work' or a 'service in the name of/on behalf of the people.' In Christian tradition it means the participation of the People of God in 'the work of God'" (*Catechism*, 1069).

Exercise

- The exercise on page four encourages the participants to write their own prayers of "remembering" and "petition."

Take it home

- Before the end of the evening, ask the small groups to talk once more about how they plan to take home and live what they have learned. Refer to the reflections, and suggest they use them to help apply the core message of this booklet. Invite them to make concrete and realistic plans. Allow a few minutes for this discussion.

Conclusion

- Go to slide 11 and announce the time and place of the next gathering.
- Go to slide 12 and invite everyone to pray the closing prayer aloud. (You can make copies of the prayer, found on page 29 of this guide, or use the prayer of Blessed John XXIII on page 5.) You can, instead, invite the group to offer spontaneous prayer. You may also close the evening with the dismissal song on the CD.

Session Plan for Reflection Booklet **22**

How Does the Church Pray?

Content summary

The people, places, and actions of the liturgy (based on articles 1135–1209 in the *Catechism of the Catholic Church*)

- The Liturgy of the Word is an integral part of each liturgy celebrated by the church.
- Sunday is the principal day for the celebration of the Eucharist because it is the day of the resurrection. It is the pre-eminent day of the liturgical assembly, the day of the Christian family, and the day of joy and rest from work. Sunday is "the foundation and kernel of the whole liturgical year."
- The Church, "in the course of the year...unfolds the whole mystery of Christ from his Incarnation and Nativity through his Ascension, to Pentecost and the expectation of the blessed hope of the coming of the Lord."
- The diverse liturgical traditions or rites, legitimately recognized, manifest the catholicity of the Church because they signify and communicate the same mystery of Christ.

Preparation

- Read through the booklet once, reflectively. Reread it and make your own notes.
- Read through the session plan and become comfortable with the format.
- For more background, read articles 1135–1209 of the *Catechism*. Mark and look up any unfamiliar words.
- Decide if and when you will do the exercise found after the material for pages six and seven. Have the materials needed.
- See pages 12–13 in this guide for other steps for preparation and materials needed.

Opening

- After introductions, if the number of participants is ten or more, ask them to form small groups. If the assembly is a large one, have each group choose a spokesperson.
- Have PowerPoint slide 1 (the cover illustration) on the screen as you begin.
- Open with the prayer found on page 4 in the introductory section of this guide. You may make copies for the participants. Or use the gathering song on the CD.

- Use the Question of the Week approach to break open the word of God from the Sunday liturgy (see 6 on page 12). Then continue with the *Growing Faith* booklet.

Pages two and three

Read and reflect

- Make sure everyone has a copy of the booklet.
- Ask the participants to read pages two and three of the booklet quietly. Tell them they will have a few minutes to do so (about five minutes).
- Invite them to mark the text when they read something that strikes them.

Share it with others

- Read the reflection on slide 2 and/or the reflection(s) provided in the booklet. Ask participants to discuss these questions in their small groups as a means of applying what they have learned in the text. Encourage them to take notes in their booklets. Give them several minutes to do all this. You may wish to play quiet music in the background during this time.
- If the assembly is large, ask the spokesperson of each small group to share a summary of the group's discussion with the larger group. Write on the board a short version or outline of all the responses.
- Use the PowerPoint slide 3 to provide the group with a visual of a Scripture passage. Open your Bibles to Ephesians 5:18–19, and select a few verses to read aloud. How does this Scripture passage relate to what you have just read and discussed?
- Pause for a few moments of silence, then go to the illustration on slide 4, which is also found in the booklet. Ask the participants to look at the illustration. On the back cover you will find a reference for this illustration, from Scripture or the *Catechism*, that may assist you. Music has long been a vital part of Catholic worship. When we sing, our hearts are lifted and our spirits soar! Liturgical music is an important part of our spiritual journey. "One cannot find anything more religious and more joyful in sacred celebrations than a whole congregation expressing its faith and devotion in song. Therefore the active participation of the whole people, which is shown in singing, is to be carefully promoted" (*Instruction on Music in the Liturgy*, 16).
- Invite feedback and general conversation about this illustration and its commentary (about five minutes).

Break

Pages four and five

The illustration

- Show the illustration on slide 5, which is the same as the one in the booklet. Invite the participants to look at the illustration. Ask questions such as: What do the words on this banner or ribbon tell you? Why do you think the ribbon is continuous, i.e., without a beginning or end?

- Refer to the quote on the back cover. "In the liturgical year, various aspects of the Paschal Mystery unfold." The liturgical year runs from the First Sunday of Advent through to the Feast of Christ the King. This leads back to Advent, when the liturgical year begins all over again. The central celebration of the year is the Resurrection of Christ. "Beginning with the Easter Triduum as its source of light, the new age of the Resurrection fills the whole liturgical year with its brilliance" (*Catechism*, 1171, 1168).

- Invite feedback on this illustration and its commentary (about 5 minutes).

Read and reflect

- Ask participants to read pages four and five. Follow the same process for reading and reflection that you used for the first pages.

Share it with others

- Read the reflection on slide 6 and/or the reflection(s) provided in the booklet. Use the same format for group discussion and sharing as you did for the previous pages.

- Use PowerPoint slide 7 to provide the group with a visual of a Scripture passage. Open your Bibles to Colossians 2:6, and select a few verses to read aloud. How does this Scripture passage relate to what you have just read and discussed?

- Pause for a few moments of silence.

Pages six and seven

Personal experience

- Ask everyone to look at the heading on page six, "Where do we celebrate?" Invite them to reflect on these questions: What images and feelings does the word "celebrate" evoke in me? What memories are linked to it? What makes a celebration memorable?

Read and reflect

- Again, follow the same process for reading and reflection on pages six and seven.

Share it with others

- Read the reflection on slide 8 and/or the reflection(s) provided in the booklet. Use the same format for group discussion and sharing.

- Use PowerPoint slide 9 to provide the group with a visual of a Scripture passage. Open your Bibles to Colossians 3:16, and select a few verses to read aloud. How does this Scripture passage relate to what you have just read and discussed?

- Pause for a few moments of silence, then ask the participants to look at the illustration on slide 10, which is the same as the one on these pages. Refer to the quote on the back cover. This icon depicts St. Stephen, an early martyr of the church. Icons and other sacred art have long been a part of Catholic worship and representative of the different cultures that make up the Church. They inspire prayer and remind us of the various ways to follow Christ. We do not worship the icon, but we honor the person(s) represented and, in so doing, draw closer to God.

Exercise

- On page four the exercise asks participants to make a chart. Invite everyone to complete this activity as a way to "personalize" the liturgical year.

Take it home

- Before the end of the evening, ask the small groups to talk once more about how they plan to take home and live what they have learned. Refer to the reflections, and suggest they use them to help apply the core message of this booklet. Invite them to make concrete and realistic plans. Allow a few minutes for this discussion.

Conclusion

- Go to slide 11 and announce the time and place of the next gathering.

- Go to slide 12 and invite everyone to pray the closing prayer aloud. (You can make copies of the prayer, found on page 29 of this guide, or use the prayer of Blessed John XXIII on page 5.) You can, instead, invite the group to offer spontaneous prayer. You may also close the evening with the dismissal song on the CD.

Session Plan for Reflection Booklet **23**

How Do We Begin Life in the Church?

Content summary

Baptism (based on articles 1212–1284 in the *Catechism of the Catholic Church*)

- Christian initiation is accomplished in three sacraments: baptism, which is the beginning of new life; confirmation, which strengthens that life; and the Eucharist, which nourishes disciples with Christ's body and blood for their transformation in Christ.

- The essential rite of baptism consists in immersing the candidate in water or pouring water on his or her head, while invoking of the Holy Trinity: the Father, the Son, and the Holy Spirit.

- Those who die for the faith, those who are catechumens, and all those who—without knowing the church but acting under the inspiration of grace—seek God sincerely and strive to fulfill God's will, can all be saved, even if they have not been baptized.

- Baptism is a grace and a gift of God that does not presuppose any human merit. Infants are baptized in the faith of the Church. Older children and adults are baptized or accepted into the church after a period of preparation called the catechumenate.

Preparation

- Read through the booklet once, reflectively. Reread it and make your own notes.
- Read through the session plan and become comfortable with the format.
- For more background, read articles 1212–1284 of the *Catechism*. Mark and look up any unfamiliar words.
- Decide if and when you will do the exercise found after the material for pages six and seven. Have the materials needed.
- See pages 12–13 in this guide for other steps for preparation and materials needed.

Opening

- After introductions, if the number of participants is ten or more, ask them to form small groups. If the assembly is a large one, have each group choose a spokesperson.
- Have PowerPoint slide 1 (the cover illustration) on the screen as you begin.
- Open with the prayer found on page 4 in the introductory section of this guide. You may make copies for the participants. Or use the gathering song on the CD.
- Use the Question of the Week approach to break open the word of God from the Sunday liturgy (see 6 on page 12). Then continue with the *Growing Faith* booklet.

Pages two and three

Read and reflect

- Make sure everyone has a copy of the booklet.
- Ask the participants to read pages two and three of the booklet quietly. Tell them they will have a few minutes to do so (about five minutes).
- Invite them to mark the text when they read something that strikes them.

Share it with others

- Read the reflection on slide 2 and/or the reflection(s) provided in the booklet. Ask participants to discuss these questions in their small groups as a means of applying what they have learned in the text. Encourage them to take notes in their booklets. Give them several minutes to do all this. You may wish to play quiet music in the background during this time.
- If the assembly is large, ask the spokesperson of each small group to share a summary of the group's discussion with the larger group. Write on the board a short version or outline of all the responses.
- Use the PowerPoint slide 3 to provide the group with a visual of a Scripture passage. Open your Bibles to 1 Corinthians 12:13, and select a few verses to read aloud. How does this Scripture passage relate to what you have just read and discussed?
- Pause for a few moments of silence, then go to the illustration on slide 4, which is also found in the booklet. Ask the participants to look at the illustration. On the back cover you will find a reference for this illustration, from Scripture or the *Catechism*, that may assist you. Water is a symbol of baptism. Why is that? Because water is vital for life. It is elemental and essential. For that reason water has a unique significance for us as it has had for people throughout the ages.
- Invite feedback and general conversation about this illustration and its commentary (about five minutes).

Break

Pages four and five

The illustration

- Show the illustration on slide 5, which is the same as the one in the booklet. Invite the participants to look at the illustration. Ask questions such as: Look at each of the elements of the picture. What does the candle symbolize for you? The towel? (and so on).

- Refer to the quote on the back cover. "Always, baptism is seen as connected with faith." The baptismal font is where our Christian lives begin. There we are immersed in the waters of baptism. We enter into the death of the Lord so as to rise with him. Baptism initiates us into the paschal mystery of Christ.

- Invite feedback on this illustration and its commentary (about 5 minutes).

Read and reflect

- Ask participants to read pages four and five. Follow the same process for reading and reflection that you used for the first pages.

Share it with others

- Read the reflection on slide 6 and/or the reflection(s) provided in the booklet. Use the same format for group discussion and sharing as you did for the previous pages.

- Use PowerPoint slide 7 to provide the group with a visual of a Scripture passage. Open your Bibles to 2 Corinthians 5:17, and select a few verses to read aloud. How does this Scripture passage relate to what you have just read and discussed?

- Pause for a few moments of silence.

Pages six and seven

Personal experience

- Ask everyone to look at the heading on page seven, "The necessity of baptism." Invite them to reflect on these questions: What if your child or a good friend died without being baptized? What would happen to them? What difference has baptism made in your life?

Read and reflect

- Again, follow the same process for reading and reflection on pages six and seven.

Share it with others

- Read the reflection on slide 8 and/or the reflection(s) provided in the booklet. Use the same format for group discussion and sharing.
- Use PowerPoint slide 9 to provide the group with a visual of a Scripture passage. Open your Bibles to Acts 2:38, and select a few verses to read aloud. How does this Scripture passage relate to what you have just read and discussed?
- Pause for a few moments of silence, then ask the participants to look at the illustration on slide 10, which is the same as the one on these pages. Refer to the quote on the back cover. The essential moment in the rite of baptism is being immersed in water or having the water poured over us, while the minister (priest or deacon) says the words: "(Name), I baptize you in the name of the Father, and of the Son, and of the Holy Spirit." This ancient sacramental sign is a sacred one. The indelible seal of baptism identifies us as Christians, and commits us to living as a disciple of Christ.

Exercise

- Read the story of Paul and Silas in prison (Acts 16:16–40) as suggested in the exercise on page two. Invite the small groups to write the story as a news article, with a catchy headline and first sentence.

Take it home

- Before the end of the evening, ask the small groups to talk once more about how they plan to take home and live what they have learned. Refer to the reflections, and suggest they use them to help apply the core message of this booklet. Invite them to make concrete and realistic plans. Allow a few minutes for this discussion.

Conclusion

- Go to slide 11 and announce the time and place of the next gathering.
- Go to slide 12 and invite everyone to pray the closing prayer aloud. (You can make copies of the prayer, found on page 29 of this guide, or use the prayer of Blessed John XXIII on page 5.) You can, instead, invite the group to offer spontaneous prayer. You may also close the evening with the dismissal song on the CD.

Session Plan for Reflection Booklet **24**

How Does the Holy Spirit Strengthen Us?

Content summary

Confirmation (based on articles 1285–1321 in the *Catechism of the Catholic Church*)

- Confirmation perfects baptismal grace. This sacrament gives the Holy Spirit in order to incorporate us more firmly into Christ, strengthen our bond with the church, and help us bear witness to the Christian faith.
- In the East confirmation is administered immediately after baptism and is followed by participation in the Eucharist. This tradition highlights the unity of the three sacraments of Christian initiation.
- Candidates for confirmation who have attained the age of reason must profess the faith, be in the state of grace, and have the intention of receiving the sacrament. They should be prepared to assume the role of disciple and witness to Christ, both within the ecclesial community and in temporal affairs.
- The essential rite of confirmation is anointing the forehead of the baptized with sacred chrism (in the East other senseorgans as well), together with the laying on of the minister's hand and the words: Be sealed with the Gift of the Holy Spirit.

Preparation

- Read through the booklet once, reflectively. Reread it and make your own notes.
- Read through the session plan and become comfortable with the format.
- For more background, read articles 1285–1321 of the *Catechism*. Mark and look up any unfamiliar words.
- Decide if and when you will do the exercise found after the material for pages six and seven. Have the materials needed.
- See pages 12–13 in this guide for other steps for preparation and materials needed.

Opening

- After introductions, if the number of participants is ten or more, ask them to form small groups. If the assembly is a large one, have each group choose a spokesperson.

- Have PowerPoint slide 1 (the cover illustration) on the screen as you begin.
- Open with the prayer found on page 4 in the introductory section of this guide. You may make copies for the participants. Or use the gathering song on the CD.
- Use the Question of the Week approach to break open the word of God from the Sunday liturgy (see 6 on page 12). Then continue with the *Growing Faith* booklet.

Pages two and three

Read and reflect

- Make sure everyone has a copy of the booklet.
- Ask the participants to read pages two and three of the booklet quietly. Tell them they will have a few minutes to do so (about five minutes).
- Invite them to mark the text when they read something that strikes them.

Share it with others

- Read the reflection on slide 2 and/or the reflection(s) provided in the booklet. Ask participants to discuss these questions in their small groups as a means of applying what they have learned in the text. Encourage them to take notes in their booklets. Give them several minutes to do all this. You may wish to play quiet music in the background during this time.
- If the assembly is large, ask the spokesperson of each small group to share a summary of the group's discussion with the larger group. Write on the board a short version or outline of all the responses.
- Use the PowerPoint slide 3 to provide the group with a visual of a Scripture passage. Open your Bibles to John 16:13, and select a few verses to read aloud. How does this Scripture passage relate to what you have just read and discussed?
- Pause for a few moments of silence, then go to the illustration on slide 4, which is also found in the booklet. Ask the participants to look at the illustration. On the back cover you will find a reference for this illustration, from Scripture or the *Catechism*, that may assist you. Being "in Christ" brings a wonderful joy to our lives, as the people in this group show. We find inner strength to live as Jesus taught. The Spirit is our guide and helper, as Jesus himself promised.
- Invite feedback and general conversation about this illustration and its commentary (about five minutes).

Break

Pages four and five

The illustration

- Show the illustration on slide 5, which is the same as the one in the booklet. Invite the participants to look at the illustration. Ask questions such as: What are each of the people in the picture doing? What is the bishop holding? What is the meaning of anointing with oil?

- Refer to the quote on the back cover. "The ordinary minister of confirmation is the bishop." When we are confirmed, we celebrate the power of the Holy Spirit in our lives. This image shows a bishop confirming, which is the custom in the western tradition. In the East, the priest confirms at the time of baptism. "Jesus answered, 'Very truly I tell you, no one can enter the kingdom of God without being born of water and Spirit. What is born of the flesh is flesh, and what is born of the Spirit is spirit'" (John 3:5–6).

- Invite feedback on this illustration and its commentary (about 5 minutes).

Read and reflect

- Ask participants to read pages four and five. Follow the same process for reading and reflection that you used for the first pages.

Share it with others

- Read the reflection on slide 6 and/or the reflection(s) provided in the booklet. Use the same format for group discussion and sharing as you did for the previous pages.

- Use PowerPoint slide 7 to provide the group with a visual of a Scripture passage. Open your Bibles to John 14:16, and select a few verses to read aloud. How does this Scripture passage relate to what you have just read and discussed?

- Pause for a few moments of silence.

Pages six and seven

Personal experience

- Ask everyone to look at the heading on page six, "Who is confirmed?" Invite them to reflect on these questions: What do you remember about your confirmation? How have the gifts of the Spirit played a part in your daily life?

Read and reflect

- Again, follow the same process for reading and reflection on pages six and seven.

Share it with others

- Read the reflection on slide 8 and/or the reflection(s) provided in the booklet. Use the same format for group discussion and sharing.
- Use PowerPoint slide 9 to provide the group with a visual of a Scripture passage. Open your Bibles to 1 Timothy 6:12, and select a few verses to read aloud. How does this Scripture passage relate to what you have just read and discussed?
- Pause for a few moments of silence, then ask the participants to look at the illustration on slide 10, which is the same as the one on these pages. Refer to the quote on the back cover. This young woman represents those who celebrate the sacrament of confirmation. As they grow older, they need to establish a firm foundation for their faith. When we are young, we set the patterns for Christian living that will last a lifetime. Openness to the gifts of the Spirit makes us more aware of God's action in our lives.

Exercise

- Ask the small groups to complete the exercise on page five. This activity will help participants apply the gifts of the sacrament to daily life.

Take it home

- Before the end of the evening, ask the small groups to talk once more about how they plan to take home and live what they have learned. Refer to the reflections, and suggest they use them to help apply the core message of this booklet. Invite them to make concrete and realistic plans. Allow a few minutes for this discussion.

Conclusion

- Go to slide 11 and announce the time and place of the next gathering.
- Go to slide 12 and invite everyone to pray the closing prayer aloud. (You can make copies of the prayer, found on page 29 of this guide, or use the prayer of Blessed John XXIII on page 5.) You can, instead, invite the group to offer spontaneous prayer. You may also close the evening with the dismissal song on the CD.

Session Plan for Reflection Booklet **25**

How Is Our Christian Initiation Completed?

Content summary

Eucharist (based on articles 1322–1419 in the *Catechism of the Catholic Church*)

- The Eucharist is the heart and the summit of the church's life.
- The Eucharistic Celebration always includes: the proclamation of the word of God; thanksgiving to God the Father for all his benefits, above all the gift of his Son; the consecration of bread and wine; and participation in the liturgical banquet by receiving the Lord's body and blood.
- Christ himself, acting through the ministry of the priests, offers the eucharistic sacrifice.
- The essential signs of the sacrament are wheat bread and grape wine, on which the blessing of the Holy Spirit is invoked. The priest pronounces the words of consecration spoken by Jesus during the Last Supper: "This is my body which will be given up for you…. This is the cup of my blood."

Preparation

- Read through the booklet once, reflectively. Reread it and make your own notes.
- Read through the session plan and become comfortable with the format.
- For more background, read articles 1322–1419 of the *Catechism*. Mark and look up any unfamiliar words.
- Decide if and when you will do the exercise found after the material for pages six and seven. Have the materials needed.
- See pages 12–13 in this guide for other steps for preparation and materials needed.

Opening

- After introductions, if the number of participants is ten or more, ask them to form small groups. If the assembly is a large one, have each group choose a spokesperson.
- Have PowerPoint slide 1 (the cover illustration) on the screen as you begin.

- Open with the prayer found on page 4 in the introductory section of this guide. You may make copies for the participants. Or use the gathering song on the CD.
- Use the Question of the Week approach to break open the word of God from the Sunday liturgy (see 6 on page 12). Then continue with the *Growing Faith* booklet.

Pages two and three

Read and reflect

- Make sure everyone has a copy of the booklet.
- Ask the participants to read pages two and three of the booklet quietly. Tell them they will have a few minutes to do so (about five minutes).
- Invite them to mark the text when they read something that strikes them.

Share it with others

- Read the reflection on slide 2 and/or the reflection(s) provided in the booklet. Ask participants to discuss these questions in their small groups as a means of applying what they have learned in the text. Encourage them to take notes in their booklets. Give them several minutes to do all this. You may wish to play quiet music in the background during this time.
- If the assembly is large, ask the spokesperson of each small group to share a summary of the group's discussion with the larger group. Write on the board a short version or outline of all the responses.
- Use the PowerPoint slide 3 to provide the group with a visual of a Scripture passage. Open your Bibles to 1 Corinthians 11:26, and select a few verses to read aloud. How does this Scripture passage relate to what you have just read and discussed?
- Pause for a few moments of silence, then go to the illustration on slide 4, which is also found in the booklet. Ask the participants to look at the illustration. On the back cover you will find a reference for this illustration, from Scripture or the *Catechism*, that may assist you. The signs of bread and wine are ancient ones in the human family. They are staples of our lives. Because they are so basic and elemental, we discover the fullness of meaning that Christ intended when we bring them to this celebration. "You cause the grass to grow for the cattle, and plants for people to use, to bring forth food from the earth, and wine to gladden the human heart, oil to make the face shine, and bread to strengthen the human heart" (Psalm 104:14–15). The bread and wine symbolize Christ's gift of himself in the paschal mystery.
- Invite feedback and general conversation about this illustration and its commentary (about five minutes).

Break

Pages four and five

The illustration

- Show the illustration on slide 5, which is the same as the one in the booklet. Invite the participants to look at the illustration. Ask questions such as: What does a family meal have to do with Eucharist? Are your meal times happy and blessed times together? What can you do to make them more so?
- Refer to the quote on the back cover. "They partook of food with glad and generous hearts." When we are in Christ, we give ourselves to each other, especially in moments like this shared meal. These are ways for us to extend and expand the celebration of the Eucharist. We recall the Lord's Supper and God's love for us, and offer God thanksgiving for his loving kindness.
- Invite feedback on this illustration and its commentary (about 5 minutes).

Read and reflect

- Ask participants to read pages four and five. Follow the same process for reading and reflection that you used for the first pages.

Share it with others

- Read the reflection on slide 6 and/or the reflection(s) provided in the booklet. Use the same format for group discussion and sharing as you did for the previous pages.
- Use PowerPoint slide 7 to provide the group with a visual of a Scripture passage. Open your Bibles to Philippians 1:3, and select a few verses to read aloud. How does this Scripture passage relate to what you have just read and discussed?
- Pause for a few moments of silence.

Pages six and seven

Personal experience

- Ask everyone to look at the heading on page six, "Real presence." Invite them to reflect on these questions: Where and how have you experienced Christ's presence? How have you tried to be Christ's presence for others?

Read and reflect

- Again, follow the same process for reading and reflection on pages six and seven.

Share it with others

- Read the reflection on slide 8 and/or the reflection(s) provided in the booklet. Use the same format for group discussion and sharing.

- Use PowerPoint slide 9 to provide the group with a visual of a Scripture passage. Open your Bibles to Matthew 26:26, and select a few verses to read aloud. How does this Scripture passage relate to what you have just read and discussed?

- Pause for a few moments of silence, then ask the participants to look at the illustration on slide 10, which is the same as the one on these pages. Refer to the quote on the back cover. The Eucharist is the most central activity of the church. In communion we become what we receive: the body of Christ. We celebrate Christ's substantial (real) presence in the Eucharist, and are united with one another in the Church. This isn't merely an activity, though; it's also our very identity as Catholics.

Exercise

- Working in small groups, the participants can do the exercise on page six. It asks them to open their hearts to those in the church who may feel "left out."

Take it home

- Before the end of the evening, ask the small groups to talk once more about how they plan to take home and live what they have learned. Refer to the reflections, and suggest they use them to help apply the core message of this booklet. Invite them to make concrete and realistic plans. Allow a few minutes for this discussion.

Conclusion

- Go to slide 11 and announce the time and place of the next gathering.

- Go to slide 12 and invite everyone to pray the closing prayer aloud. (You can make copies of the prayer, found on page 29 of this guide, or use the prayer of Blessed John XXIII on page 5.) You can, instead, invite the group to offer spontaneous prayer. You may also close the evening with the dismissal song on the CD.

Session Plan for Reflection Booklet **26**

How Does God Offer Unending Forgiveness?

Content summary

Reconciliation (based on articles 1420–1498 in the *Catechism of the Catholic Church*)
- The forgiveness of sins committed after baptism is conferred by the sacrament of penance or reconciliation.
- Our return to God, called conversion and repentance, includes sorrow for and abhorrence of sins committed, and the firm purpose of sinning no more.
- The essential rite of the sacrament of penance consists of our repentance, our confession of sins to the priest, our intention to make reparation and do works of reparation, and the priest's words of absolution and blessing.
- The spiritual effects of the sacrament of reconciliation are: reconciliation with God by which we recover grace; reconciliation with the Church; peace and serenity of conscience and spiritual consolation; and growth in our spiritual life.

Preparation

- Read through the booklet once, reflectively. Reread it and make your own notes.
- Read through the session plan and become comfortable with the format.
- For more background, read articles 1420–1498 of the *Catechism*. Mark and look up any unfamiliar words.
- Decide if and when you will do the exercise found after the material for pages six and seven. Have the materials needed.
- See pages 12–13 in this guide for other steps for preparation and materials needed.

Opening

- After introductions, if the number of participants is ten or more, ask them to form small groups. If the assembly is a large one, have each group choose a spokesperson.
- Have PowerPoint slide 1 (the cover illustration) on the screen as you begin.
- Open with the prayer found on page 4 in the introductory section of this guide. You may make copies for the participants. Or use the gathering song on the CD.

• Use the Question of the Week approach to break open the word of God from the Sunday liturgy (see 6 on page 12). Then continue with the *Growing Faith* booklet.

Pages two and three

Read and reflect

• Make sure everyone has a copy of the booklet.
• Ask the participants to read pages two and three of the booklet quietly. Tell them they will have a few minutes to do so (about five minutes).
• Invite them to mark the text when they read something that strikes them.

Share it with others

• Read the reflection on slide 2 and/or the reflection(s) provided in the booklet. Ask participants to discuss these questions in their small groups as a means of applying what they have learned in the text. Encourage them to take notes in their booklets. Give them several minutes to do all this. You may wish to play quiet music in the background during this time.
• If the assembly is large, ask the spokesperson of each small group to share a summary of the group's discussion with the larger group. Write on the board a short version or outline of all the responses.
• Use the PowerPoint slide 3 to provide the group with a visual of a Scripture passage. Open your Bibles to 1 John 1:8, and select a few verses to read aloud. How does this Scripture passage relate to what you have just read and discussed?
• Pause for a few moments of silence, then go to the illustration on slide 4, which is also found in the booklet. Ask the participants to look at the illustration. On the back cover you will find a reference for this illustration, from Scripture or the *Catechism*, that may assist you. Every church now has a special room devoted to the sacrament of reconciliation. Here we sit with a priest and humbly pray for God's forgiveness. We confess our failings and express our repentance, and ask for guidance in our spiritual life. Through the sacraments we receive pardon from God's mercy and are reconciled with the Church.
• Invite feedback and general conversation about this illustration and its commentary (about five minutes).

Break

Pages four and five

The illustration

- Show the illustration on slide 5, which is the same as the one in the booklet. Invite the participants to look at the illustration. Ask questions such as: Do you find it difficult or easy to confess your sins? Why? Do you see this sacrament as a means for growing spiritually by discussing your progress (or lack of it)?
- Refer to the quote on the back cover. "I absolve you from your sins." Confession of our sins helps us see the reality of our actions and amend our lives. Part of our spiritual journey involves sharing our faith, including the ways in which we have failed to grow and love. We do this in a special way in the sacrament of reconciliation, so as to receive the spiritual guidance we need.
- Invite feedback on this illustration and its commentary (about 5 minutes).

Read and reflect

- Ask participants to read pages four and five. Follow the same process for reading and reflection that you used for the first pages.

Share it with others

- Read the reflection on slide 6 and/or the reflection(s) provided in the booklet. Use the same format for group discussion and sharing as you did for the previous pages.
- Use PowerPoint slide 7 to provide the group with a visual of a Scripture passage. Open your Bibles to 1 John 1:9, and select a few verses to read aloud. How does this Scripture passage relate to what you have just read and discussed?
- Pause for a few moments of silence.

Pages six and seven

Personal experience

- Ask everyone to look at the heading on page six, "Making amends." Invite them to reflect on these questions: When you've hurt someone, how do you make amends for it? When you let an argument cause a break with someone, how do you feel? How does "making up" make a difference?

Read and reflect

- Again, follow the same process for reading and reflection on pages six and seven.

Share it with others

- Read the reflection on slide 8 and/or the reflection(s) provided in the booklet. Use the same format for group discussion and sharing.
- Use PowerPoint slide 9 to provide the group with a visual of a Scripture passage. Open your Bibles to 1 Corinthians 12:26, and select a few verses to read aloud. How does this Scripture passage relate to what you have just read and discussed?
- Pause for a few moments of silence, then ask the participants to look at the illustration on slide 10, which is the same as the one on these pages. Refer to the quote on the back cover. The story of the prodigal son illustrated how God feels toward us. When we repent of our failings, we are embraced by God in loving forgiveness. God waits at the door to welcome us home. God deeply desires that we return to him with our whole heart.

Exercise

- Invite the participants to do the exercise on page two. It asks them how to correct their course on their journey of faith. This whole booklet is an excellent preparation for a reconciliation service.

Take it home

- Before the end of the evening, ask the small groups to talk once more about how they plan to take home and live what they have learned. Refer to the reflections, and suggest they use them to help apply the core message of this booklet. Invite them to make concrete and realistic plans. Allow a few minutes for this discussion.

Conclusion

- Go to slide 11 and announce the time and place of the next gathering.
- Go to slide 12 and invite everyone to pray the closing prayer aloud. (You can make copies of the prayer, found on page 29 of this guide, or use the prayer of Blessed John XXIII on page 5.) You can, instead, invite the group to offer spontaneous prayer. You may also close the evening with the dismissal song on the CD.

Session Plan for Reflection Booklet **27**

How Does God Heal Us?

Content summary

Anointing of the sick (based on articles 1499–1532 in the *Catechism of the Catholic Church*)

- The sacrament of anointing of the sick gives a special grace to Christians suffering from the difficulties of grave illness or old age.
- Each time a Christian falls seriously ill, he or she may receive the anointing of the sick, and again when the illness worsens.
- The celebration of the anointing of the sick consists essentially in the anointing of the forehead and hands of the sick person (in the Roman tradition) or of other parts of the body (in the eastern tradition). The anointing is accompanied by the liturgical prayer of the celebrant, asking for the special grace of this sacrament.
- The special grace of the anointing of the sick unites the sick person to the passion of Christ, and provides strength, peace, and courage to endure the sufferings of illness or old age.

Preparation

- Read through the booklet once, reflectively. Reread it and make your own notes.
- Read through the session plan and become comfortable with the format.
- For more background, read articles 1499–1532 of the *Catechism*. Mark and look up any unfamiliar words.
- Decide if and when you will do the exercise found after the material for pages six and seven. Have the materials needed.
- See pages 12–13 in this guide for other steps for preparation and materials needed.

Opening

- After introductions, if the number of participants is ten or more, ask them to form small groups. If the assembly is a large one, have each group choose a spokesperson.
- Have PowerPoint slide 1 (the cover illustration) on the screen as you begin.
- Open with the prayer found on page 4 in the introductory section of this guide. You may make copies for the participants. Or use the gathering song on the CD.

- Use the Question of the Week approach to break open the word of God from the Sunday liturgy (see 6 on page 12). Then continue with the *Growing Faith* booklet.

Pages two and three

Read and reflect

- Make sure everyone has a copy of the booklet.
- Ask the participants to read pages two and three of the booklet quietly. Tell them they will have a few minutes to do so (about five minutes).
- Invite them to mark the text when they read something that strikes them.

Share it with others

- Read the reflection on slide 2 and/or the reflection(s) provided in the booklet. Ask participants to discuss these questions in their small groups as a means of applying what they have learned in the text. Encourage them to take notes in their booklets. Give them several minutes to do all this. You may wish to play quiet music in the background during this time.
- If the assembly is large, ask the spokesperson of each small group to share a summary of the group's discussion with the larger group. Write on the board a short version or outline of all the responses.
- Use the PowerPoint slide 3 to provide the group with a visual of a Scripture passage. Open your Bibles to James 5:14, and select a few verses to read aloud. How does this Scripture passage relate to what you have just read and discussed?
- Pause for a few moments of silence, then go to the illustration on slide 4, which is also found in the booklet. Ask the participants to look at the illustration. On the back cover you will find a reference for this illustration, from Scripture or the *Catechism*, that may assist you. The sign of oil, represented here by the containers of oil, is an ancient and powerful one. Oil has been used for ages to strengthen and heal athletes and sick persons. It also symbolizes inner strength and beauty, and helps us prepare for our journey and "fight the good fight" of faith.
- Invite feedback and general conversation about this illustration and its commentary (about five minutes).

Break

Pages four and five

The illustration

- Show the illustration on slide 5, which is the same as the one in the booklet. Invite the participants to look at the illustration. Ask questions such as: Describe the image to yourself, using a story, symbols, or a memory. What do you think is the meaning of the picture (besides the obvious one)? What part does each person play?
- Refer to the quote on the back cover. "Christ makes [the] miseries [of the sick] his own." Like Christ, the church has a special love for the sick and miserable. We treat them as our sisters and brothers, providing hospitals, nursing homes, AIDS shelters, homeless assistance, and many other forms of service.
- Invite feedback on this illustration and its commentary (about 5 minutes).

Read and reflect

- Ask participants to read pages four and five. Follow the same process for reading and reflection that you used for the first pages.

Share it with others

- Read the reflection on slide 6 and/or the reflection(s) provided in the booklet. Use the same format for group discussion and sharing as you did for the previous pages.
- Use PowerPoint slide 7 to provide the group with a visual of a Scripture passage. Open your Bibles to 1 Corinthians 12:26, and select a few verses to read aloud. How does this Scripture passage relate to what you have just read and discussed?
- Pause for a few moments of silence.

Pages six and seven

Personal experience

- Ask everyone to look at the second heading on page six, "The fruits of this sacrament." Invite them to reflect on these questions: Have you ever been present at an anointing? What was the experience like? Why do you think Christ gave us this sacrament?

Read and reflect

- Again, follow the same process for reading and reflection on pages six and seven.

Share it with others

- Read the reflection on slide 8 and/or the reflection(s) provided in the booklet. Use the same format for group discussion and sharing.
- Use PowerPoint slide 9 to provide the group with a visual of a Scripture passage. Open your Bibles to Luke 6:19, and select a few verses to read aloud. How does this Scripture passage relate to what you have just read and discussed?
- Pause for a few moments of silence, then ask the participants to look at the illustration on slide 10, which is the same as the one on these pages. Refer to the quote on the back cover. The church offers the sacrament of the anointing of the sick to continue the ministry of Christ among us. The priest anoints the forehead and hands of the sick person with oil, while praying for the special grace of the sacraments. In this sacrament we are given the grace to "carry our cross" and find meaning in suffering and death.

Exercise

- Invite participants to briefly write or draw about a healing in their own lives or the life of a loved one. If time allows, ask them to share their work in small groups.

Take it home

- Before the end of the evening, ask the small groups to talk once more about how they plan to take home and live what they have learned. Refer to the reflections, and suggest they use them to help apply the core message of this booklet. Invite them to make concrete and realistic plans. Allow a few minutes for this discussion.

Conclusion

- Go to slide 11 and announce the time and place of the next gathering.
- Go to slide 12 and invite everyone to pray the closing prayer aloud. (You can make copies of the prayer, found on page 29 of this guide, or use the prayer of Blessed John XXIII on page 5.) You can, instead, invite the group to offer spontaneous prayer. You may also close the evening with the dismissal song on the CD.

Session Plan for Reflection Booklet **28**

How Does God Consecrate for the Service of the Church?

Content summary

Holy orders (based on articles 1533–1600 in the *Catechism of the Catholic Church*)

- The whole church is a priestly people. Through baptism we all share in the priesthood of Christ, called the "common priesthood of the faithful."
- The ministerial priesthood differs in essence from the common priesthood of the faithful because it confers a sacred power for the service of the faithful. Ordained ministers exercise their service by teaching, divine worship, and pastoral governance.
- Since the beginning, the ordained ministry has been conferred and exercised in three degrees: that of bishops, that of priests, and that of deacons.
- The sacrament of holy orders is celebrated by the laying on of hands, followed by a solemn prayer of consecration asking God to grant the ordinand the graces of the Holy Spirit required for his ministry.

Preparation

- Read through the booklet once, reflectively. Reread it and make your own notes.
- Read through the session plan and become comfortable with the format.
- For more background, read articles 1533–1600 of the *Catechism*. Mark and look up any unfamiliar words.
- Decide if and when you will do the exercise found after the material for pages six and seven. Have the materials needed.
- See pages 12–13 in this guide for other steps for preparation and materials needed.

Opening

- After introductions, if the number of participants is ten or more, ask them to form small groups. If the assembly is a large one, have each group choose a spokesperson.
- Have PowerPoint slide 1 (the cover illustration) on the screen as you begin.

- Open with the prayer found on page 4 in the introductory section of this guide. You may make copies for the participants. Or use the gathering song on the CD.
- Use the Question of the Week approach to break open the word of God from the Sunday liturgy (see 6 on page 12). Then continue with the *Growing Faith* booklet.

Pages two and three

Read and reflect

- Make sure everyone has a copy of the booklet.
- Ask the participants to read pages two and three of the booklet quietly. Tell them they will have a few minutes to do so (about five minutes).
- Invite them to mark the text when they read something that strikes them.

Share it with others

- Read the reflection on slide 2 and/or the reflection(s) provided in the booklet. Ask participants to discuss these questions in their small groups as a means of applying what they have learned in the text. Encourage them to take notes in their booklets. Give them several minutes to do all this. You may wish to play quiet music in the background during this time.
- If the assembly is large, ask the spokesperson of each small group to share a summary of the group's discussion with the larger group. Write on the board a short version or outline of all the responses.
- Use the PowerPoint slide 3 to provide the group with a visual of a Scripture passage. Open your Bibles to Mark 10:45, and select a few verses to read aloud. How does this Scripture passage relate to what you have just read and discussed?
- Pause for a few moments of silence, then go to the illustration on slide 4, which is also found in the booklet. Ask the participants to look at the illustration. On the back cover you will find a reference for this illustration, from Scripture or the *Catechism*, that may assist you. Being part of a parish, committed with heart and soul, is how we live out our Christian Catholic calling. Our pastor, the head of the parish, is given the gift of love and service. He is to be the example of Christ in our midst. For we, too, are called to serve.
- Invite feedback and general conversation about this illustration and its commentary (about five minutes).

Break

Pages four and five

The illustration

- Invite the participants to look at the illustration on slide 5, which is the same as the one in the booklet. Ask questions such as: Look at the elements of the picture, e.g., the vestments, the host, the chalice, and the priest himself. What do these elements mean to you? What do they say about the man in the picture?
- Refer to the quote on the back cover. "The ministerial priesthood is a means by which Christ builds up and leads his church." Christ is the only true priest, and all others are his ministers. Just as the apostles received their mandate from Christ, so do the bishops, priests, and deacons in today's church. Each of them carries out the duties that belong to their role in the community.
- Invite feedback on this illustration and its commentary (about 5 minutes).

Read and reflect

- Ask participants to read pages four and five. Follow the same process for reading and reflection that you used for the first pages.

Share it with others

- Read the reflection on slide 6 and/or the reflection(s) provided in the booklet. Use the same format for group discussion and sharing as you did for the previous pages.
- Use PowerPoint slide 7 to provide the group with a visual of a Scripture passage. Open your Bibles to 1 Timothy 6:11, and select a few verses to read aloud. How does this Scripture passage relate to what you have just read and discussed?
- Pause for a few moments of silence.

Pages six and seven

Personal experience

- Ask everyone to look at the heading on page six, "How we ordain." Invite them to reflect on these questions: How do you perceive the sacrament of holy orders? Is there a priest or deacon who has made a positive impact on your life and spiritual growth?

Read and reflect

- Again, follow the same process for reading and reflection on pages six and seven.

Share it with others

- Read the reflection on slide 8 and/or the reflection(s) provided in the booklet. Use the same format for group discussion and sharing.
- Use PowerPoint slide 9 to provide the group with a visual of a Scripture passage. Open your Bibles to Ephesians 4:11, and select a few verses to read aloud. How does this Scripture passage relate to what you have just read and discussed?
- Pause for a few moments of silence, then ask the participants to look at the illustration on slide 10, which is the same as the one on these pages. Refer to the quote on the back cover. The essential moment of ordination is the laying on of hands by a bishop and the prayer of consecration. In this way the church asks God for the special gifts the newly ordained will need to serve the church.

Exercise

- Ask the participants to work in groups and prepare a litany of the saints, that focuses on ordained ministers and women who made a significant impact on the church, e.g., St. John Neumann, St. Teresa of Avila, St. John Bosco, St. Elizabeth Seton.

Take it home

- Before the end of the evening, ask the small groups to talk once more about how they plan to take home and live what they have learned. Refer to the reflections, and suggest they use them to help apply the core message of this booklet. Invite them to make concrete and realistic plans. Allow a few minutes for this discussion.

Conclusion

- Go to slide 11 and announce the time and place of the next gathering.
- Go to slide 12 and invite everyone to pray the closing prayer aloud. (You can make copies of the prayer, found on page 29 of this guide, or use the prayer of Blessed John XXIII on page 5.) You can, instead, invite the group to offer spontaneous prayer. You may also close the evening with the dismissal song on the CD.

Session Plan for Reflection Booklet **29**

How Is Love Blessed and Celebrated?

Content summary

Matrimony (based on articles 1601–1666 in the *Catechism of the Catholic Church*)

- In the marriage covenant a man and a woman form with each other an intimate communion of life and love. The Creator has founded and endowed it with its own special laws. By its very nature marriage is for the good of the couple, as well as the generation and education of children.
- Marriage is based on the will of a man and woman to give themselves, each to the other, mutually and definitively, in order to live a covenant of faithful and fruitful love.
- Unity, permanence, and openness to fertility are essential to marriage.
- The Christian home is the place where children receive their first proclamation of the faith. For this reason the family home is rightly called "the domestic church," a community of grace and prayer, a school of human virtues and of Christian charity.

Preparation

- Read through the booklet once, reflectively. Reread it and make your own notes.
- Read through the session plan and become comfortable with the format.
- For more background, read articles 1601–1666 of the *Catechism*. Mark and look up any unfamiliar words.
- Decide if and when you will do the exercise found after the material for pages six and seven. Have the materials needed.
- See pages 12–13 in this guide for other steps for preparation and materials needed.

Opening

- After introductions, if the number of participants is ten or more, ask them to form small groups. If the assembly is a large one, have each group choose a spokesperson.
- Have PowerPoint slide 1 (the cover illustration) on the screen as you begin.

- Open with the prayer found on page 4 in the introductory section of this guide. You may make copies for the participants. Or use the gathering song on the CD.
- Use the Question of the Week approach to break open the word of God from the Sunday liturgy (see 6 on page 12). Then continue with the *Growing Faith* booklet.

Pages two and three

Read and reflect

- Make sure everyone has a copy of the booklet.
- Ask the participants to read pages two and three of the booklet quietly. Tell them they will have a few minutes to do so (about five minutes).
- Invite them to mark the text when they read something that strikes them.

Share it with others

- Read the reflection on slide 2 and/or the reflection(s) provided in the booklet. Ask participants to discuss these questions in their small groups as a means of applying what they have learned in the text. Encourage them to take notes in their booklets. Give them several minutes to do all this. You may wish to play quiet music in the background during this time.
- If the assembly is large, ask the spokesperson of each small group to share a summary of the group's discussion with the larger group. Write on the board a short version or outline of all the responses.
- Use the PowerPoint slide 3 to provide the group with a visual of a Scripture passage. Open your Bibles to Genesis 1:28, and select a few verses to read aloud. How does this Scripture passage relate to what you have just read and discussed?
- Pause for a few moments of silence, then go to the illustration on slide 4, which is also found in the booklet. Ask the participants to look at the illustration. On the back cover you will find a reference for this illustration, from Scripture or the *Catechism*, that may assist you. Each of our homes is a domestic church in which children and guests find a model of faith and an example of Christian living. This is the particular vocation of married couples. Prayer is first learned in the home, faith is first implanted, and love is first known.
- Invite feedback and general conversation about this illustration and its commentary (about five minutes).

Break

Pages four and five

The illustration

- Invite the participants to look at the illustration on slide 5, which is the same as the one in the booklet. Ask questions such as: What memories and feelings does this image evoke? What do the candles symbolize? Why does marriage require unconditional, undivided love?
- Refer to the quote on the back cover. "The spouses…mutually confer the sacrament of matrimony." When we marry another person, we are called to give ourselves generously and completely, to be tender, loving, and caring. Such love requires that we die to ourselves in Christ, i.e., that we give up selfish habits and place the good of our spouse before our own happiness.
- Invite feedback on this illustration and its commentary (about 5 minutes).

Read and reflect

- Ask participants to read pages four and five. Follow the same process for reading and reflection that you used for the first pages.

Share it with others

- Read the reflection on slide 6 and/or the reflection(s) provided in the booklet. Use the same format for group discussion and sharing as you did for the previous pages.
- Use PowerPoint slide 7 to provide the group with a visual of a Scripture passage. Open your Bibles to 1 Corinthians 7:16, and select a few verses to read aloud. How does this Scripture passage relate to what you have just read and discussed?
- Pause for a few moments of silence.

Pages six and seven

Personal experience

- Ask everyone to look at the heading on page seven, "Households of faith." Ask questions such as: What do you think makes a home a "household of faith"? What areas do you think your own household could make progress in? What do you think your strong points are?

Read and reflect

- Again, follow the same process for reading and reflection on pages six and seven.

Share it with others

- Read the reflection on slide 8 and/or the reflection(s) provided in the booklet. Use the same format for group discussion and sharing.
- Use PowerPoint slide 9 to provide the group with a visual of a Scripture passage. Open your Bibles to Ephesians 6:1, and select a few verses to read aloud. How does this Scripture passage relate to what you have just read and discussed?
- Pause for a few moments of silence, then ask the participants to look at the illustration on slide 10, which is the same as the one on these pages. Refer to the quote on the back cover. The Christian home is a place where neighbors, relatives, surprise guests, and even strangers feel welcome. Christ is the host in our homes. Christ sets the table. We welcome all in Christ's name.

Exercise

- Ask the participants to pair up with someone in the group whom they don't know very well. Have them take some time to get to know each other better, e.g., what their hobbies and interests are, what they do for a living, about their children, and so on.

Take it home

- Before the end of the evening, ask the small groups to talk once more about how they plan to take home and live what they have learned. Refer to the reflections, and suggest they use them to help apply the core message of this booklet. Invite them to make concrete and realistic plans. Allow a few minutes for this discussion.

Conclusion

- Go to slide 11 and announce the time and place of the next gathering.
- Go to slide 12 and invite everyone to pray the closing prayer aloud. (You can make copies of the prayer, found on page 29 of this guide, or use the prayer of Blessed John XXIII on page 5.) You can, instead, invite the group to offer spontaneous prayer. You may also close the evening with the dismissal song on the CD.

Session Plan for Reflection Booklet **30**

What Makes Us Free?

Content summary

We are destined for God (based on articles 1691–1748 in the *Catechism of the Catholic Church*)

- Endowed with a spiritual soul, with intellect and free will, as human persons we are from the moment of our conception destined to be with God and to enjoy eternal happiness.
- We are obliged to follow the moral law, which urges us "to do what is good and avoid what is evil." This law makes itself heard in our conscience.
- The Beatitudes help us respond to the desire for happiness that God has placed in our hearts.
- Our right to the exercise of freedom, especially in religious and moral matters, is an inalienable requirement of human dignity. However, this does not give us the right to say or do anything we please.

Preparation

- Read through the booklet once, reflectively. Reread it and make your own notes.
- Read through the session plan and become comfortable with the format.
- For more background, read articles 1691–1748 of the *Catechism*. Mark and look up any unfamiliar words.
- Decide if and when you will do the exercise found after the material for pages six and seven. Have the materials needed.
- See pages 12–13 in this guide for other steps for preparation and materials needed.

Opening

- After introductions, if the number of participants is ten or more, ask them to form small groups. If the assembly is a large one, have each group choose a spokesperson.
- Have PowerPoint slide 1 (the cover illustration) on the screen as you begin.
- Open with the prayer found on page 4 in the introductory section of this Gguide. You may make copies for the participants. Or use the gathering song on the CD.

- Use the Question of the Week approach to break open the word of God from the Sunday liturgy (see 6 on page 12). Then continue with the *Growing Faith* booklet.

Pages two and three

Read and reflect

- Make sure everyone has a copy of the booklet.
- Ask the participants to read pages two and three of the booklet quietly. Tell them they will have a few minutes to do so (about five minutes).
- Invite them to mark the text when they read something that strikes them.

Share it with others

- Read the reflection on slide 2 and/or the reflection(s) provided in the booklet. Ask participants to discuss these questions in their small groups as a means of applying what they have learned in the text. Encourage them to take notes in their booklets. Give them several minutes to do all this. You may wish to play quiet music in the background during this time.
- If the assembly is large, ask the spokesperson of each small group to share a summary of the group's discussion with the larger group. Write on the board a short version or outline of all the responses.
- Use the PowerPoint slide 3 to provide the group with a visual of a Scripture passage. Open your Bibles to Matthew 5:8, and select a few verses to read aloud. How does this Scripture passage relate to what you have just read and discussed?
- Pause for a few moments of silence, then go to the illustration on slide 4, which is also found in the booklet. Ask the participants to look at the illustration. On the back cover you will find a reference for this illustration, from Scripture or the *Catechism*, that may assist you. We humans are destined to live with God, to follow the pathway for life that God sets for us. Because we are created in God's image each of us has great dignity, and is made for love and a share in divine life. Christ teaches us to respect the dignity of others and help one another follow our calling.
- Invite feedback and general conversation about this illustration and its commentary (about five minutes).

Break

Pages four and five

The illustration

- Invite the participants to look at the illustration on slide 5, which is the same as the one in the booklet. Ask questions such as: What does this image say to you? What do you think this picture has to do with the headings on these pages (human destiny, be happy!, and so on)? What does it mean to you to "be happy"?
- Refer to the quote on the back cover. "We all want to live happily." We all make choices. What we choose is terribly important because on our choices rest our good and the good of the world. Christ teaches us to choose humility, peace, and mercy.
- Invite feedback on this illustration and its commentary (about 5 minutes).

Read and reflect

- Ask participants to read pages four and five. Follow the same process for reading and reflection that you used for the first pages.

Share it with others

- Read the reflection on slide 6 and/or the reflection(s) provided in the booklet. Use the same format for group discussion and sharing as you did for the previous pages.
- Use PowerPoint slide 7 to provide the group with a visual of a Scripture passage. Open your Bibles to Romans 6:16, and select a few verses to read aloud. How does this Scripture passage relate to what you have just read and discussed?
- Pause for a few moments of silence.

Pages six and seven

Personal experience

- Ask everyone to look at the heading on page six, "Human freedom." Invite them to reflect on these questions: What might it be like if we didn't have the freedom to make choices, if we were all the same and did the same things? How precious is your freedom to you? What are some of the responsibilities that accompany freedom?

Read and reflect

- Again, follow the same process for reading and reflection on pages six and seven.

Share it with others

- Read the reflection on slide 8 and/or the reflection(s) provided in the booklet. Use the same format for group discussion and sharing.
- Use PowerPoint slide 9 to provide the group with a visual of a Scripture passage. Open your Bibles to Galatians 5:1, and select a few verses to read aloud. How does this Scripture passage relate to what you have just read and discussed?
- Pause for a few moments of silence, then ask the participants to look at the illustration on slide 10, which is the same as the one on these pages. Refer to the quote on the back cover. Each of us is called to work for justice and liberation. Martin Luther King, Jr., responded to his calling even though it cost him his life. What are the conditions you see around you now that call you to become involved?

Exercise

- Invite the participants to do the exercise on page two, working together in small groups. Ask them to make their choice of action simple, concrete, and feasible.

Take it home

- Before the end of the evening, ask the small groups to talk once more about how they plan to take home and live what they have learned. Refer to the reflections, and suggest they use them to help apply the core message of this booklet. Invite them to make concrete and realistic plans. Allow a few minutes for this discussion.

Conclusion

- Go to slide 11 and announce the time and place of the next gathering.
- Go to slide 12 and invite everyone to pray the closing prayer aloud. (You can make copies of the prayer, found on page 29 of this guide, or use the prayer of Blessed John XXIII on page 5.) You can, instead, invite the group to offer spontaneous prayer. You may also close the evening with the dismissal song on the CD.

Session Plan for Reflection Booklet **31**

What Is Right and Wrong and How Do We Know?

Content summary

Morality and conscience (based on articles 1749–1802 in the *Catechism of the Catholic Church*)

- Certain concrete acts are always wrong to choose, because their choice entails a disorder of the will, i.e., a moral evil. We may not do evil to achieve a good result.
- Conscience is a judgment of reason by which we as human persons recognize the moral quality of a concrete act.
- A well-formed conscience is upright and truthful. It formulates its judgments according to reason and the true good willed by the Creator. Each of us must use the means to form our consciences.
- The word of God is a light for our path. We need to make God's word our own through faith and prayer, and put it into practice. This is how moral conscience is formed.

Preparation

- Read through the booklet once, reflectively. Reread it and make your own notes.
- Read through the session plan and become comfortable with the format.
- For more background, read articles 1749–1802 of the *Catechism*. Mark and look up any unfamiliar words.
- Decide if and when you will do the exercise found after the material for pages six and seven. Have the materials needed.
- See pages 12–13 in this guide for other steps for preparation and materials needed.

Opening

- After introductions, if the number of participants is ten or more, ask them to form small groups. If the assembly is a large one, have each group choose a spokesperson.
- Have PowerPoint slide 1 (the cover illustration) on the screen as you begin.

- Open with the prayer found on page 4 in the introductory section of this guide. You may make copies for the participants. Or use the gathering song on the CD.
- Use the Question of the Week approach to break open the word of God from the Sunday liturgy (see 6 on page 12). Then continue with the *Growing Faith* booklet.

Pages two and three

Read and reflect

- Make sure everyone has a copy of the booklet.
- Ask the participants to read pages two and three of the booklet quietly. Tell them they will have a few minutes to do so (about five minutes).
- Invite them to mark the text when they read something that strikes them.

Share it with others

- Read the reflection on slide 2 and/or the reflection(s) provided in the booklet. Ask participants to discuss these questions in their small groups as a means of applying what they have learned in the text. Encourage them to take notes in their booklets. Give them several minutes to do all this. You may wish to play quiet music in the background during this time.
- If the assembly is large, ask the spokesperson of each small group to share a summary of the group's discussion with the larger group. Write on the board a short version or outline of all the responses.
- Use the PowerPoint slide 3 to provide the group with a visual of a Scripture passage. Open your Bibles to Romans 2:14–15, and select a few verses to read aloud. How does this Scripture passage relate to what you have just read and discussed?
- Pause for a few moments of silence, then go to the illustration on slide 4, which is also found in the booklet. Ask the participants to look at the illustration. On the back cover you will find a reference for this illustration, from Scripture or the *Catechism*, that may assist you. It is in our nature as human beings to be loving and follow the law. When we don't, we violate our own nature. Hitler is an example of this. His thoughts and actions, his influence on others, and the tragic events that resulted, violated what we know to be true and good. "The human person has always looked for, and found, truths of a higher order. For our intellect is not confined to the range of what can be observed by the senses. Our intellectual nature finds at last its perfection in wisdom, which gently draws our mind to look for and love what is true and good" (*Church in the Modern World*, 15).
- Invite feedback and general conversation about this illustration and its commentary (about five minutes).

Break

Pages four and five

The illustration

- Invite the participants to look at the illustration on slide 5, which is the same as the one in the booklet. Ask questions such as: What might the girl be praying about? How often do you pray for guidance or help in making choices?
- Refer to the quote on the back cover. "It is important to hear and follow the voice of conscience." The gospels often relate that Jesus spent time alone in prayer. He prayed before each major decision or action of his life, from choosing his apostles to accepting his cross. Likewise, we should make time in our day for prayer, especially when we need the direction or strength to listen to our conscience.
- Invite feedback on this illustration and its commentary (about 5 minutes).

Read and reflect

- Ask participants to read pages four and five. Follow the same process for reading and reflection that you used for the first pages.

Share it with others

- Read the reflection on slide 6 and/or the reflection(s) provided in the booklet. Use the same format for group discussion and sharing as you did for the previous pages.
- Use PowerPoint slide 7 to provide the group with a visual of a Scripture passage. Open your Bibles to Mark 6:45–46, and select a few verses to read aloud. How does this Scripture passage relate to what you have just read and discussed?
- Pause for a few moments of silence.

Pages six and seven

Personal experience

- Ask everyone to look at the heading on page six, "Forming conscience." Invite them to reflect on these questions: What do these words mean to you? What steps or actions do you take to form your conscience? Do they include being aware of the injustices around you?

Read and reflect

- Again, follow the same process for reading and reflection on pages six and seven.

Share it with others

- Read the reflection on slide 8 and/or the reflection(s) provided in the booklet. Use the same format for group discussion and sharing.

- Use PowerPoint slide 9 to provide the group with a visual of a Scripture passage. Open your Bibles to Ephesians 4:22–24, and select a few verses to read aloud. How does this Scripture passage relate to what you have just read and discussed?

- Pause for a few moments of silence, then ask the participants to look at the illustration on slide 10, which is the same as the one on these pages. Refer to the quote on the back cover. Our conscience awakens us to sin and selfishness around us. But we must form and shape our conscience before the Lord's cross and in the light of the gospel. How do we do that?

Exercise

- Working in small groups have the participants make a list of Catholic Christians who had to make "tough" decisions in their lives, and why/how they were able to make those decisions.

Take it home

- Before the end of the evening, ask the small groups to talk once more about how they plan to take home and live what they have learned. Refer to the reflections, and suggest they use them to help apply the core message of this booklet. Invite them to make concrete and realistic plans. Allow a few minutes for this discussion.

Conclusion

- Go to slide 11 and announce the time and place of the next gathering.

- Go to slide 12 and invite everyone to pray the closing prayer aloud. (You can make copies of the prayer, found on page 29 of this guide, or use the prayer of Blessed John XXIII on page 5.) You can, instead, invite the group to offer spontaneous prayer. You may also close the evening with the dismissal song on the CD.

Session Plan for Reflection Booklet **32**

How Do We Cultivate Virtues?

Content summary

Faith, hope, and charity (based on articles 1803–1845 in the *Catechism of the Catholic Church*)

- Virtue is a habitual and firm disposition to do good.
- The three theological virtues are faith, hope, and charity. They inform all the moral virtues and give them life.
- Moral virtues can be grouped around the four cardinal virtues: prudence, justice, fortitude, and temperance.
- The seven gifts of the Holy Spirit bestowed upon Christians are wisdom, understanding, counsel, fortitude, knowledge, piety, and awe in the face of God's generous goodness.

Preparation

- Read through the booklet once, reflectively. Reread it and make your own notes.
- Read through the session plan and become comfortable with the format.
- For more background, read articles 1803–1845 of the *Catechism*. Mark and look up any unfamiliar words.
- Decide if and when you will do the exercise found after the material for pages six and seven. Have the materials needed.
- See pages 12–13 in this guide for other steps for preparation and materials needed.

Opening

- After introductions, if the number of participants is ten or more, ask them to form small groups. If the assembly is a large one, have each group choose a spokesperson.
- Have PowerPoint slide 1 (the cover illustration) on the screen as you begin.
- Open with the prayer found on page 4 in the introductory section of this guide. You may make copies for the participants. Or use the gathering song on the CD.
- Use the Question of the Week approach to break open the word of God from the Sunday liturgy (see 6 on page 12). Then continue with the *Growing Faith* booklet.

Pages two and three

Read and reflect

- Make sure everyone has a copy of the booklet.
- Ask the participants to read pages two and three of the booklet quietly. Tell them they will have a few minutes to do so (about five minutes).
- Invite them to mark the text when they read something that strikes them.

Share it with others

- Read the reflection on slide 2 and/or the reflection(s) provided in the booklet. Ask participants to discuss these questions in their small groups as a means of applying what they have learned in the text. Encourage them to take notes in their booklets. Give them several minutes to do all this. You may wish to play quiet music in the background during this time.
- If the assembly is large, ask the spokesperson of each small group to share a summary of the group's discussion with the larger group. Write on the board a short version or outline of all the responses.
- Use the PowerPoint slide 3 to provide the group with a visual of a Scripture passage. Open your Bibles to Sirach 19:20, and select a few verses to read aloud. How does this Scripture passage relate to what you have just read and discussed?
- Pause for a few moments of silence, then go to the illustration on slide 4, which is also found in the booklet. Ask the participants to look at the illustration. On the back cover you will find a reference for this illustration, from Scripture or the *Catechism*, that may assist you. We grow in our faith and in wisdom. This is why catechesis is a lifelong journey of faith. Like this "wisdom figure" we gradually become wise. "Conversion to Jesus Christ implies walking in his footsteps. Catechesis must, therefore, transmit to the disciples the attitudes of the Master himself. The disciples thus undertake a journey of interior transformation, in which, by participating in the paschal mystery of the Lord, 'they pass from the old man to the new man who has been made perfect in Christ'" (GDC, 85).
- Invite feedback and general conversation about this illustration and its commentary (about five minutes).

Break

The illustration

- Invite the participants to look at the illustration on slide 5, which is the same as the one in the booklet. Ask questions such as: What is this picture about? What do these athletes have to do with practicing virtue?
- Refer to the quote on the back cover. "[We] should always ask for this grace of light and strength." Virtue brings about a certain spiritual balance within us. Like an athlete practicing hard for a game, we need to practice virtue until it becomes a habit. The theological virtues, in particular, are central to our Christian life.
- Invite feedback on this illustration and its commentary (about 5 minutes).

Read and reflect

- Ask participants to read pages four and five. Follow the same process for reading and reflection that you used for the first pages.

Share it with others

- Read the reflection on slide 6 and/or the reflection(s) provided in the booklet. Use the same format for group discussion and sharing as you did for the previous pages.
- Use PowerPoint slide 7 to provide the group with a visual of a Scripture passage. Open your Bibles to Psalm 118:14, and select a few verses to read aloud. How does this Scripture passage relate to what you have just read and discussed?
- Pause for a few moments of silence.

Pages six and seven

Personal experience

- Ask everyone to look at the heading on page seven, "The spirit of love." Invite them to reflect on these questions: When and how have you experienced the action of the Spirit of love in your life? How did you respond? How did it affect others around you?

Read and reflect

- Again, follow the same process for reading and reflection on pages six and seven.

Share it with others

- Read the reflection on slide 8 and/or the reflection(s) provided in the booklet. Use the same format for group discussion and sharing.
- Use PowerPoint slide 9 to provide the group with a visual of a Scripture passage. Open your Bibles to Colossians 3:14, and select a few verses to read aloud. How does this Scripture passage relate to what you have just read and discussed?
- Pause for a few moments of silence, then ask the participants to look at the illustration on slide 10, which is the same as the one on these pages. Refer to the quote on the back cover. Like the saint, we are all called to open our arms to others in charity, as Christ did on the cross. The cross is a symbol of right living and loving, of selflessness and self-giving. As St. Paul wrote, charity is the greatest virtue.

Exercise

- Invite the participants to work in small groups to prepare an advertisement for someone to teach virtue. List requirements, references, and so on.

Take it home

- Before the end of the evening, ask the small groups to talk once more about how they plan to take home and live what they have learned. Refer to the reflections, and suggest they use them to help apply the core message of this booklet. Invite them to make concrete and realistic plans. Allow a few minutes for this discussion.

Conclusion

- Go to slide 11 and announce the time and place of the next gathering.
- Go to slide 12 and invite everyone to pray the closing prayer aloud. (You can make copies of the prayer, found on page 29 of this guide, or use the prayer of Blessed John XXIII on page 5.) You can, instead, invite the group to offer spontaneous prayer. You may also close the evening with the dismissal song on the CD.

Session Plan for Reflection Booklet **33**

What Is Sin?

Content summary

Sin is missing the mark (based on articles 1846–1876 in the *Catechism of the Catholic Church*)

- Sin is a word, deed, or desire contrary to the eternal law. We turn away from God in a disobedience contrary to the obedience of Christ.
- To deliberately choose—that is, both knowingly and willingly—something gravely contrary to the divine law and to the ultimate purpose of human life is to commit a mortal sin.
- Venial sin is a moral disorder reparable by charity.
- The repetition of sins—even venial ones—wears down our wills and can lead us to commit more serious sins.

Preparation

- Read through the booklet once, reflectively. Reread it and make your own notes.
- Read through the session plan and become comfortable with the format.
- For more background, read articles 1846–1876 of the *Catechism*. Mark and look up any unfamiliar words.
- Decide if and when you will do the exercise found after the material for pages six and seven. Have the materials needed.
- See pages 12–13 in this guide for other steps for preparation and materials needed.

Opening

- After introductions, if the number of participants is ten or more, ask them to form small groups. If the assembly is a large one, have each group choose a spokesperson.
- Have PowerPoint slide 1 (the cover illustration) on the screen as you begin.
- Open with the prayer found on page 4 in the introductory section of this guide. You may make copies for the participants. Or use the gathering song on the CD.
- Use the Question of the Week approach to break open the word of God from the Sunday liturgy (see 6 on page 12). Then continue with the *Growing Faith* booklet.

Pages two and three

Read and reflect

- Make sure everyone has a copy of the booklet.
- Ask the participants to read pages two and three of the booklet quietly. Tell them they will have a few minutes to do so (about five minutes).
- Invite them to mark the text when they read something that strikes them.

Share it with others

- Read the reflection on slide 2 and/or the reflection(s) provided in the booklet. Ask participants to discuss these questions in their small groups as a means of applying what they have learned in the text. Encourage them to take notes in their booklets. Give them several minutes to do all this. You may wish to play quiet music in the background during this time.
- If the assembly is large, ask the spokesperson of each small group to share a summary of the group's discussion with the larger group. Write on the board a short version or outline of all the responses.
- Use the PowerPoint slide 3 to provide the group with a visual of a Scripture passage. Open your Bibles to Psalm 51:4, and select a few verses to read aloud. How does this Scripture passage relate to what you have just read and discussed?
- Pause for a few moments of silence, then go to the illustration on slide 4, which is also found in the booklet. Ask the participants to look at the illustration. On the back cover you will find a reference for this illustration, from Scripture or the *Catechism*, that may assist you. When an archer uses a bent arrow, he or she cannot hit the target they are aiming for. In a similar way, sin causes us to miss the mark set for us by God.
- Invite feedback and general conversation about this illustration and its commentary (about five minutes).

Break

Pages four and five

The illustration

- Invite the participants to look at the illustration on slide 5, which is the same as the one in the booklet. Ask questions such as: Look at each of the persons in the picture. What memories, feelings, or beliefs do they present to you? How do you think the picture of the father with his son relates to our topic?
- Refer to the quote on the back cover. "Father, I have sinned against heaven." God's love for us is like that of this father for his son, or a mother for her child. God's love is full of compassion and the desire that we remain close. God forgives us and takes us back over and over again.
- Invite feedback on this illustration and its commentary (about 5 minutes).

Read and reflect

- Ask participants to read pages four and five. Follow the same process for reading and reflection that you used for the first pages.

Share it with others

- Read the reflection on slide 6 and/or the reflection(s) provided in the booklet. Use the same format for group discussion and sharing as you did for the previous pages.
- Use PowerPoint slide 7 to provide the group with a visual of a Scripture passage. Open your Bibles to Luke 15:24, and select a few verses to read aloud. How does this Scripture passage relate to what you have just read and discussed?
- Pause for a few moments of silence.

Pages six and seven

Personal experience

- Ask everyone to look at the heading on page seven, "Capital sins." Invite them to reflect on these questions: Which of the capital sins do I struggle against most or am most tempted to give in to? What do I do to overcome it? How can the sacrament of reconciliation help me in this struggle?

Read and reflect

- Again, follow the same process for reading and reflection on pages six and seven.

Share it with others

- Read the reflection on slide 8 and/or the reflection(s) provided in the booklet. Use the same format for group discussion and sharing.
- Use PowerPoint slide 9 to provide the group with a visual of a Scripture passage. Open your Bibles to Mark 3:5, and select a few verses to read aloud. How does this Scripture passage relate to what you have just read and discussed?
- Pause for a few moments of silence, then ask the participants to look at the illustration on slide 10, which is the same as the one on these pages. Refer to the quote on the back cover. The capital sins nibble away at our inner lives, causing us to become callous toward sin or even indifferent to it. Greed is one of those sins, and perhaps the most insidious. The rich do not see how rich they really are, and often they do not care about the sufferings of others.

Exercise

- Working together in small groups the participants can write a brief modern version of one of the parables, e.g., the prodigal son or the rich man and Lazarus.

Take it home

- Before the end of the evening, ask the small groups to talk once more about how they plan to take home and live what they have learned. Refer to the reflections, and suggest they use them to help apply the core message of this booklet. Invite them to make concrete and realistic plans. Allow a few minutes for this discussion.

Conclusion

- Go to slide 11 and announce the time and place of the next gathering.
- Go to slide 12 and invite everyone to pray the closing prayer aloud. (You can make copies of the prayer, found on page 29 of this guide, or use the prayer of Blessed John XXIII on page 5.) You can, instead, invite the group to offer spontaneous prayer. You may also close the evening with the dismissal song on the CD.

Session Plan for Reflection Booklet **34**

How Should We Live as a Community?

Content summary

Society and human dignity (based on articles 1877–1948 in the *Catechism of the Catholic Church*)

- There is a likeness between the unity of the Trinity and the community that we as human persons should establish among ourselves.
- Society ought to promote the exercise of virtue, not obstruct it. Society should be organized around a sense of value and the common good of all.
- Public authority is exercised legitimately only if it is committed to the common good of society. To attain this it must employ morally acceptable means.
- The equal dignity of human persons requires that we reduce excessive social and economic inequalities.

Preparation

- Read through the booklet once, reflectively. Reread it and make your own notes.
- Read through the session plan and become comfortable with the format.
- For more background, read articles 1877–1948 of the *Catechism*. Mark and look up any unfamiliar words.
- Decide if and when you will do the exercise found after the material for pages six and seven. Have the materials needed.
- See pages 12–13 in this guide for other steps for preparation and materials needed.

Opening

- After introductions, if the number of participants is ten or more, ask them to form small groups. If the assembly is a large one, have each group choose a spokesperson.
- Have PowerPoint slide 1 (the cover illustration) on the screen as you begin.
- Open with the prayer found on page 4 in the introductory section of this guide. You may make copies for the participants. Or use the gathering song on the CD.

- Use the Question of the Week approach to break open the word of God from the Sunday liturgy (see 6 on page 12). Then continue with the *Growing Faith* booklet.

Pages two and three

Read and reflect

- Make sure everyone has a copy of the booklet.
- Ask the participants to read pages two and three of the booklet quietly. Tell them they will have a few minutes to do so (about five minutes).
- Invite them to mark the text when they read something that strikes them.

Share it with others

- Read the reflection on slide 2 and/or the reflection(s) provided in the booklet. Ask participants to discuss these questions in their small groups as a means of applying what they have learned in the text. Encourage them to take notes in their booklets. Give them several minutes to do all this. You may wish to play quiet music in the background during this time.
- If the assembly is large, ask the spokesperson of each small group to share a summary of the group's discussion with the larger group. Write on the board a short version or outline of all the responses.
- Use the PowerPoint slide 3 to provide the group with a visual of a Scripture passage. Open your Bibles to Philippians 2:3, and select a few verses to read aloud. How does this Scripture passage relate to what you have just read and discussed?
- Pause for a few moments of silence, then go to the illustration on slide 4, which is also found in the booklet. Ask the participants to look at the illustration. On the back cover you will find a reference for this illustration, from Scripture or the *Catechism*, that may assist you. Each of us needs to become involved in the community around us to help improve the lives of our sisters and brothers. As Jimmy Carter did with Habitat for Humanity, we too must "get our hands dirty" and help others have a happier, more dignified life. This is the mandate of the gospel.
- Invite feedback and general conversation about this illustration and its commentary (about five minutes).

Break

Pages four and five

The illustration

- Invite the participants to look at the illustration on slide 5, which is the same as the one in the booklet. Ask questions such as: Where do public authority and laws come from? Are they always right? What can we do to effect changes in law and government?
- Refer to the quote on the back cover. "The role [of authority] is to ensure the common good." Society establishes good order within it by having people who enforce the laws. Respecting these officials and following the laws voluntarily, even when no one sees us, is essential for a sound community.
- Invite feedback on this illustration and its commentary (about 5 minutes).

Read and reflect

- Ask participants to read pages four and five. Follow the same process for reading and reflection that you used for the first pages.

Share it with others

- Read the reflection on slide 6 and/or the reflection(s) provided in the booklet. Use the same format for group discussion and sharing as you did for the previous pages.
- Use PowerPoint slide 7 to provide the group with a visual of a Scripture passage. Open your Bibles to Colossians 3:12, and select a few verses to read aloud. How does this Scripture passage relate to what you have just read and discussed?
- Pause for a few moments of silence.

Pages six and seven

Personal experience

- Ask everyone to look at the second heading on page six, "Social justice." Invite them to reflect on these questions: Have you ever experienced injustice? How did that make you feel? What do the words "social justice" mean to you? What opportunities have you had—no matter how small—to make a difference in your community?

Read and reflect

- Again, follow the same process for reading and reflection on pages six and seven.

Share it with others

- Read the reflection on slide 8 and/or the reflection(s) provided in the booklet. Use the same format for group discussion and sharing.
- Use PowerPoint slide 9 to provide the group with a visual of a Scripture passage. Open your Bibles to Romans 13:12, and select a few verses to read aloud. How does this Scripture passage relate to what you have just read and discussed?
- Pause for a few moments of silence, then ask the participants to look at the illustration on slide 10, which is the same as the one on these pages. Refer to the quote on the back cover. Like these neighbors we live in society with other people. Keeping good society means being at peace, being involved in our communities, and knowing our neighbors. We want to live in a community where people love and trust each other.

Exercise

- Provide copies of newspapers and news magazines so participants can do the exercise on page seven.

Take it home

- Before the end of the evening, ask the small groups to talk once more about how they plan to take home and live what they have learned. Refer to the reflections, and suggest they use them to help apply the core message of this booklet. Invite them to make concrete and realistic plans. Allow a few minutes for this discussion.

Conclusion

- Go to slide 11 and announce the time and place of the next gathering.
- Go to slide 12 and invite everyone to pray the closing prayer aloud. (You can make copies of the prayer, found on page 29 of this guide, or use the prayer of Blessed John XXIII on page 5.) You can, instead, invite the group to offer spontaneous prayer. You may also close the evening with the dismissal song on the CD.

Session Plan for Reflection Booklet **35**

What Ever Happened to Grace?

Content summary

Grace and merit (based on articles 1949–2029 in the *Catechism of the Catholic Church*)

- The natural law is our participation in God's wisdom and goodness. It expresses the dignity of the human person and forms the basis of our fundamental rights and duties.
- The new law is the grace of the Holy Spirit received in Christ. It is expressed in the words of the gospels and celebrated in the sacraments.
- Moved by grace, we turn toward God and away from sin; this journey is called "conversion."
- Grace is the help God gives us to become God's own children, intimately connected to the love of the Trinity.

Preparation

- Read through the booklet once, reflectively. Reread it and make your own notes.
- Read through the session plan and become comfortable with the format.
- For more background, read articles 1949–2029 of the *Catechism*. Mark and look up any unfamiliar words.
- Decide if and when you will do the exercise found after the material for pages six and seven. Have the materials needed.
- See pages 12–13 in this guide for other steps for preparation and materials needed.

Opening

- After introductions, if the number of participants is ten or more, ask them to form small groups. If the assembly is a large one, have each group choose a spokesperson.
- Have PowerPoint slide 1 (the cover illustration) on the screen as you begin.

- Open with the prayer found on page 4 in the introductory section of this guide. You may make copies for the participants. Or use the gathering song on the CD.
- Use the Question of the Week approach to break open the word of God from the Sunday liturgy (see 6 on page 12). Then continue with the *Growing Faith* booklet.

Pages two and three

Read and reflect

- Make sure everyone has a copy of the booklet.
- Ask the participants to read pages two and three of the booklet quietly. Tell them they will have a few minutes to do so (about five minutes).
- Invite them to mark the text when they read something that strikes them.

Share it with others

- Read the reflection on slide 2 and/or the reflection(s) provided in the booklet. Ask participants to discuss these questions in their small groups as a means of applying what they have learned in the text. Encourage them to take notes in their booklets. Give them several minutes to do all this. You may wish to play quiet music in the background during this time.
- If the assembly is large, ask the spokesperson of each small group to share a summary of the group's discussion with the larger group. Write on the board a short version or outline of all the responses.
- Use the PowerPoint slide 3 to provide the group with a visual of a Scripture passage. Open your Bibles to Philippians 2:12–13, and select a few verses to read aloud. How does this Scripture passage relate to what you have just read and discussed?
- Pause for a few moments of silence, then go to the illustration on slide 4, which is also found in the booklet. Ask the participants to look at the illustration. On the back cover you will find a reference for this illustration, from Scripture or the *Catechism*, that may assist you. Each of us has the law written in our hearts. Each human person possesses God-given dignity, which no one can take away. How much more should we treat each other with respect, regardless of our diversity? In fact, we should celebrate that very diversity as gift.
- Invite feedback and general conversation about this illustration and its commentary (about five minutes).

Break

Pages four and five

The illustration

- Invite the participants to look at the illustration on slide 5, which is the same as the one in the booklet. Ask questions such as: Why do you think the "giver" is not seen here? What other, perhaps more valuable, things can we give than money? Do we see those in need as "out there," as separate from us, or as true sisters and brothers?

- Refer to the quote on the back cover. "The acts of religion: almsgiving, prayer, and fasting." The new law of Christ invites us to a selfless love for each other, especially for those who are poor or rejected by society in any way. We should look for ways to establish greater justice and to help our sisters and brothers in need.

- Invite feedback on this illustration and its commentary (about 5 minutes).

Read and reflect

- Ask participants to read pages four and five. Follow the same process for reading and reflection that you used for the first pages.

Share it with others

- Read the reflection on slide 6 and/or the reflection(s) provided in the booklet. Use the same format for group discussion and sharing as you did for the previous pages.

- Use PowerPoint slide 7 to provide the group with a visual of a Scripture passage. Open your Bibles to Matthew 6:2, and select a few verses to read aloud. How does this Scripture passage relate to what you have just read and discussed?

- Pause for a few moments of silence.

Pages six and seven

Personal experience

- Ask everyone to look at the heading on page six, "Grace." Invite them to reflect on these questions: What does the word "grace" mean to you? Do the life of grace and our vocation to holiness have priority in your daily life—whether you are a housewife, a lawyer, a teacher, a city worker, a waiter, and so on?

Read and reflect

- Again, follow the same process for reading and reflection on pages six and seven.

Share it with others

- Read the reflection on slide 8 and/or the reflection(s) provided in the booklet. Use the same format for group discussion and sharing.
- Use PowerPoint slide 9 to provide the group with a visual of a Scripture passage. Open your Bibles to Matthew 7:20, and select a few verses to read aloud. How does this Scripture passage relate to what you have just read and discussed?
- Pause for a few moments of silence, then ask the participants to look at the illustration on slide 10, which is the same as the one on these pages. Refer to the quote on the back cover. Joan of Arc had a keen sense of God's grace at work in her life. Like her, we all need to be aware of God's power acting within and through us. "The fruitfulness of lay people depends on their living union with Christ. This life of intimate union is maintained by the spiritual helps common to all the faithful, chiefly by active participation in the liturgy. They should not separate their union with Christ from their ordinary life, but, through the very performance of their tasks…actually promote the growth of their union with God" (*Decree on the Apostolate of Lay People*, 4).

Exercise

- Invite participants to work in small groups to do the exercise on page four. Assign one passage to each group. If time permits ask them to share their "findings."

Take it home

- Before the end of the evening, ask the small groups to talk once more about how they plan to take home and live what they have learned. Refer to the reflections, and suggest they use them to help apply the core message of this booklet. Invite them to make concrete and realistic plans. Allow a few minutes for this discussion.

Conclusion

- Go to slide 11 and announce the time and place of the next gathering.
- Go to slide 12 and invite everyone to pray the closing prayer aloud. (You can make copies of the prayer, found on page 29 of this guide, or use the prayer of Blessed John XXIII on page 5.) You can, instead, invite the group to offer spontaneous prayer. You may also close the evening with the dismissal song on the CD.

Session Plan for Reflection Booklet **36**

What Does God Want?

Content summary

The magisterium and the ten commandments (based on articles 2030–2082 in the *Catechism of the Catholic Church*)

- The precepts of the church are: you shall attend Mass on Sundays and holy days; you shall confess your sins at least once a year; you shall receive Holy Communion at least during the Easter season; you shall observe the prescribed days of fasting and abstinence; you have a duty to provide for the material needs of the church, according to your ability.
- The pope and bishops, as authentic teachers, preach to the people of God the faith which is to be believed and applied in moral life.
- The ten commandments contain a unique expression of the natural law.
- What God commands he makes possible by grace.

Preparation

- Read through the booklet once, reflectively. Reread it and make your own notes.
- Read through the session plan and become comfortable with the format.
- For more background, read articles 2030–2082 of the *Catechism*. Mark and look up any unfamiliar words.
- Decide if and when you will do the exercise found after the material for pages six and seven. Have the materials needed.
- See pages 12–13 in this guide for other steps for preparation and materials needed.

Opening

- After introductions, if the number of participants is ten or more, ask them to form small groups. If the assembly is a large one, have each group choose a spokesperson.
- Have PowerPoint slide 1 (the cover illustration) on the screen as you begin.
- Open with the prayer found on page 4 in the introductory section of this guide. You may make copies for the participants. Or use the gathering song on the CD.
- Use the Question of the Week approach to break open the word of God from the Sunday liturgy (see 6 on page 12). Then continue with the *Growing Faith* booklet.

Pages two and three

Read and reflect

- Make sure everyone has a copy of the booklet.
- Ask the participants to read pages two and three of the booklet quietly. Tell them they will have a few minutes to do so (about five minutes).
- Invite them to mark the text when they read something that strikes them.

Share it with others

- Read the reflection on slide 2 and/or the reflection(s) provided in the booklet. Ask participants to discuss these questions in their small groups as a means of applying what they have learned in the text. Encourage them to take notes in their booklets. Give them several minutes to do all this. You may wish to play quiet music in the background during this time.
- If the assembly is large, ask the spokesperson of each small group to share a summary of the group's discussion with the larger group. Write on the board a short version or outline of all the responses.
- Use the PowerPoint slide 3 to provide the group with a visual of a Scripture passage. Open your Bibles to Galatians 6:2, and select a few verses to read aloud. How does this Scripture passage relate to what you have just read and discussed?
- Pause for a few moments of silence, then go to the illustration on slide 4, which is also found in the booklet. Ask the participants to look at the illustration. On the back cover you will find a reference for this illustration, from Scripture or the *Catechism*, that may assist you. Dorothy Day was a true witness to her faith. She spoke on behalf of the poor and worked for their welfare. Her Catholic faith inspired her to do this.
- Invite feedback and general conversation about this illustration and its commentary (about five minutes).

Break

Pages four and five

The illustration

- Invite the participants to look at the illustration on slide 5, which is the same as the one in the booklet. Ask questions such as: What does this image convey to you? What does your own parish church look like? What does your parish life look like?

- Refer to the quote on the back cover. "The Christian fulfills his (or her) vocation [in the church]." Being part of a local Catholic parish, being active in parish life, and taking home with us the resources offered by the parish are ways in which we live a Christian life. The guidance of our pastors helps us, especially in difficult or challenging times.

- Invite feedback on this illustration and its commentary (about 5 minutes).

Read and reflect

- Ask participants to read pages four and five. Follow the same process for reading and reflection that you used for the first pages.

Share it with others

- Read the reflection on slide 6 and/or the reflection(s) provided in the booklet. Use the same format for group discussion and sharing as you did for the previous pages.

- Use PowerPoint slide 7 to provide the group with a visual of a Scripture passage. Open your Bibles to Ephesians 4:11–12, and select a few verses to read aloud. How does this Scripture passage relate to what you have just read and discussed?

- Pause for a few moments of silence.

Pages six and seven

Personal experience

- Ask everyone to look at the heading on page six, "Background." Invite them to reflect on these questions: What is your own background on the commandments? Did you memorize them without really learning about them? Do you have an elementary grade understanding, or adult formation on this topic?

Read and reflect

- Again, follow the same process for reading and reflection on pages six and seven.

Share it with others

- Read the reflection on slide 8 and/or the reflection(s) provided in the booklet. Use the same format for group discussion and sharing.

- Use PowerPoint slide 9 to provide the group with a visual of a Scripture passage. Open your Bibles to Exodus 31:18, and select a few verses to read aloud. How does this Scripture passage relate to what you have just read and discussed?

- Pause for a few moments of silence, then ask the participants to look at the illustration on slide 10, which is the same as the one on these pages. Refer to the quote on the back cover. The story of Moses on Mount Sinai uses figurative language to describe God giving us the commandments. In fact, this law was written in our hearts by our Creator. It is part and parcel of who we are. The commandments guide us in how to love God and one another.

Exercise

- Working in groups the participants can do the exercise on page two, which aims to help them connect the commandments with Jesus' teaching in the gospel.

Take it home

- Before the end of the evening, ask the small groups to talk once more about how they plan to take home and live what they have learned. Refer to the reflections, and suggest they use them to help apply the core message of this booklet. Invite them to make concrete and realistic plans. Allow a few minutes for this discussion.

Conclusion

- Go to slide 11 and announce the time and place of the next gathering.

- Go to slide 12 and invite everyone to pray the closing prayer aloud. (You can make copies of the prayer, found on page 29 of this guide, or use the prayer of Blessed John XXIII on page 5.) You can, instead, invite the group to offer spontaneous prayer. You may also close the evening with the dismissal song on the CD.

Session Plan for Reflection Booklet **37**

How Do We Know and Honor God?

Content summary

No strange gods: The first two commandments (based on articles 2083–2167 in the *Catechism of the Catholic Church*)

- The first commandment calls us to believe in God, to hope in God, and to love God above all else.
- Since atheism rejects or denies the existence of God, it is a sin against the first commandment.
- The second commandment enjoins us to respect the Lord's name. The name of the Lord is holy.
- The second commandment forbids every improper use of God's name. Blasphemy involves using the name of God, of Jesus Christ, of the Virgin Mary, or of the saints in an offensive way.

Preparation

- Read through the booklet once, reflectively. Reread it and make your own notes.
- Read through the session plan and become comfortable with the format.
- For more background, read articles 2083–2167 of the *Catechism*. Mark and look up any unfamiliar words.
- Decide if and when you will do the exercise found after the material for pages six and seven. Have the materials needed.
- See pages 12–13 in this guide for other steps for preparation and materials needed.

Opening

- After introductions, if the number of participants is ten or more, ask them to form small groups. If the assembly is a large one, have each group choose a spokesperson.
- Have PowerPoint slide 1 (the cover illustration) on the screen as you begin.

- Open with the prayer found on page 4 in the introductory section of this guide. You may make copies for the participants. Or use the gathering song on the CD.
- Use the Question of the Week approach to break open the word of God from the Sunday liturgy (see 6 on page 12). Then continue with the *Growing Faith* booklet.

Pages two and three

Read and reflect

- Make sure everyone has a copy of the booklet.
- Ask the participants to read pages two and three of the booklet quietly. Tell them they will have a few minutes to do so (about five minutes).
- Invite them to mark the text when they read something that strikes them.

Share it with others

- Read the reflection on slide 2 and/or the reflection(s) provided in the booklet. Ask participants to discuss these questions in their small groups as a means of applying what they have learned in the text. Encourage them to take notes in their booklets. Give them several minutes to do all this. You may wish to play quiet music in the background during this time.
- If the assembly is large, ask the spokesperson of each small group to share a summary of the group's discussion with the larger group. Write on the board a short version or outline of all the responses.
- Use the PowerPoint slide 3 to provide the group with a visual of a Scripture passage. Open your Bibles to Exodus 20:3, and select a few verses to read aloud. How does this Scripture passage relate to what you have just read and discussed?
- Pause for a few moments of silence, then go to the illustration on slide 4, which is also found in the booklet. Ask the participants to look at the illustration. On the back cover you will find a reference for this illustration, from Scripture or the *Catechism*, that may assist you. As Catholic Christians we worship, honor, and love the one, true God, and seek God alone as our complete destiny and happiness. We need to nourish our faith, hope, and love for God in our words, thoughts, and actions. Our love for God should lead us to love of all God's children, and to share the Good News. However, we also need to respect the beliefs of persons of other religions.
- Invite feedback and general conversation about this illustration and its commentary (about five minutes).

Break

The illustration

- Invite the participants to look at the illustration on slide 5, which is the same as the one in the booklet. Ask questions such as: What do these buildings symbolize for you? How might materialism affect your priorities and values?
- Refer to the quote on the back cover. "You cannot serve God and mammon." Jesus teaches we cannot love both God and money. This can be a real challenge because in our world today we tend to worship the false gods of money, fame, or power, pleasure or persons. Another practice common today is belief in magic, sorcery, or other forms of the occult, all of which is contrary to our faith.
- Invite feedback on this illustration and its commentary (about 5 minutes).

Read and reflect

- Ask participants to read pages four and five. Follow the same process for reading and reflection that you used for the first pages.

Share it with others

- Read the reflection on slide 6 and/or the reflection(s) provided in the booklet. Use the same format for group discussion and sharing as you did for the previous pages.
- Use PowerPoint slide 7 to provide the group with a visual of a Scripture passage. Open your Bibles to Matthew 6:24, and select a few verses to read aloud. How does this Scripture passage relate to what you have just read and discussed?
- Pause for a few moments of silence.

Personal experience

- Ask everyone to look at the heading on page six, "The Second Commandment." Invite them to reflect on these questions: What is your understanding of the second commandment? What does it involve besides reverencing God's name?

Read and reflect

- Again, follow the same process for reading and reflection on pages six and seven.

Share it with others

- Read the reflection on slide 8 and/or the reflection(s) provided in the booklet. Use the same format for group discussion and sharing.

- Use PowerPoint slide 9 to provide the group with a visual of a Scripture passage. Open your Bibles to Exodus 20:7, and select a few verses to read aloud. How does this Scripture passage relate to what you have just read and discussed?

- Pause for a few moments of silence, then ask the participants to look at the illustration on slide 10, which is the same as the one on these pages. Refer to the quote on the back cover. The second commandment directs us never to take God's name in vain but always use God's name with respect. In swearing an oath we call on God as our witness, the oath must be true and honest, or we commit "perjury." We also honor God in prayer. We bless ourselves in the name of God. We allow ourselves the deep quiet needed to hear the voice of God echo in the depths of our being.

Exercise

- Ask the participants to complete the exercise on page four which asks them to list the "false Gods" of today's culture and world. If there is time, they can share their lists with one another.

Take it home

- Before the end of the evening, ask the small groups to talk once more about how they plan to take home and live what they have learned. Refer to the reflections, and suggest they use them to help apply the core message of this booklet. Invite them to make concrete and realistic plans. Allow a few minutes for this discussion.

Conclusion

- Go to slide 11 and announce the time and place of the next gathering.

- Go to slide 12 and invite everyone to pray the closing prayer aloud. (You can make copies of the prayer, found on page 29 of this guide, or use the prayer of Blessed John XXIII on page 5.) You can, instead, invite the group to offer spontaneous prayer. You may also close the evening with the dismissal song on the CD.

Session Plan for Reflection Booklet **38**

How Do We Keep Holy the Lord's Day?

Content summary

Keeping holy: the third commandment (based on articles 2168–2195 in the *Catechism of the Catholic Church*)

- The ceremonial observance of the "sabbath" has been replaced by Sunday, which recalls the new creation inaugurated by the resurrection of Christ.
- We are to consider Sunday the foremost holy day of obligation in the universal Church.
- On Sundays we avoid unnecessary labor and work, allowing time for family and friends.
- Every Christian should avoid making unnecessary demands on others that would hinder them from observing the Lord's Day.

Preparation

- Read through the booklet once, reflectively. Reread it and make your own notes.
- Read through the session plan and become comfortable with the format.
- For more background, read articles 2168–2195 of the *Catechism*. Mark and look up any unfamiliar words.
- Decide if and when you will do the exercise found after the material for pages six and seven. Have the materials needed.
- See pages 12–13 in this guide for other steps for preparation and materials needed.

Opening

- After introductions, if the number of participants is ten or more, ask them to form small groups. If the assembly is a large one, have each group choose a spokesperson.
- Have PowerPoint slide 1 (the cover illustration) on the screen as you begin.
- Open with the prayer found on page 4 in the introductory section of this guide. You may make copies for the participants. Or use the gathering song on the CD.

- Use the Question of the Week approach to break open the word of God from the Sunday liturgy (see 6 on page 12). Then continue with the *Growing Faith* booklet.

Read and reflect

- Make sure everyone has a copy of the booklet.
- Ask the participants to read pages two and three of the booklet quietly. Tell them they will have a few minutes to do so (about five minutes).
- Invite them to mark the text when they read something that strikes them.

Share it with others

- Read the reflection on slide 2 and/or the reflection(s) provided in the booklet. Ask participants to discuss these questions in their small groups as a means of applying what they have learned in the text. Encourage them to take notes in their booklets. Give them several minutes to do all this. You may wish to play quiet music in the background during this time.
- If the assembly is large, ask the spokesperson of each small group to share a summary of the group's discussion with the larger group. Write on the board a short version or outline of all the responses.
- Use the PowerPoint slide 3 to provide the group with a visual of a Scripture passage. Open your Bibles to Exodus 20:8, and select a few verses to read aloud. How does this Scripture passage relate to what you have just read and discussed?
- Pause for a few moments of silence, then go to the illustration on slide 4, which is also found in the booklet. Ask the participants to look at the illustration. On the back cover you will find a reference for this illustration, from Scripture or the *Catechism*, that may assist you. We are often driven by a sense that "time is running out." We keep very busy in our modern world. Sunday is a time to let go of that desire to be on the move, and to ignore time as it were and rest in God instead. We follow the cycles of earth's seasons, each of which has a different purpose. Jesus taught that the Sabbath was a day to honor God, to do good, to save life.
- Invite feedback and general conversation about this illustration and its commentary (about five minutes).

Break

Pages four and five

The illustration

- Invite the participants to look at the illustration on slide 5, which is the same as the one in the booklet. Ask questions such as: Describe to yourself what is happening in the picture. What might this family be sharing besides a meal? What does a family meal have to do with keeping Sunday holy?
- Refer to the quote on the back cover. "Christians sanctify Sunday by devoting time…to their families." Sharing meals is a vital way for us to keep Sunday holy. The shared meal, even with very simple foods, responds to a deep yearning within us to build solidarity and bonds with one another, the body of Christ. The meal is a symbol and sign of our unity at another Sunday meal, the Eucharist. For us Catholics, nothing is more important in keeping Sunday holy than participating at Mass. The Eucharist is central to our lives as individuals and as a community.
- Invite feedback on this illustration and its commentary (about 5 minutes).

Read and reflect

- Ask participants to read pages four and five. Follow the same process for reading and reflection that you used for the first pages.

Share it with others

- Read the reflection on slide 6 and/or the reflection(s) provided in the booklet. Use the same format for group discussion and sharing as you did for the previous pages.
- Use PowerPoint slide 7 to provide the group with a visual aid. Ask members of your group to share how they invite others to join them for a cup of coffee, for lunch, or for dinner.
- Pause for a few moments of silence.

Pages six and seven

Personal experience

- Ask everyone to look at the heading on page six, "Rest." Invite them to reflect on these questions: How do you observe the Sunday rest? Why do we need it? Are there circumstances when it might be all right for you to work?

Read and reflect

- Again, follow the same process for reading and reflection on pages six and seven.

Share it with others

- Read the reflection on slide 8 and/or the reflection(s) provided in the booklet. Use the same format for group discussion and sharing.
- Use PowerPoint slide 9 to provide the group with a visual of a Scripture passage. Open your Bibles to Hebrews 10:24–25, and select a few verses to read aloud. How does this Scripture passage relate to what you have just read and discussed?
- Pause for a few moments of silence, then ask the participants to look at the illustration on slide 10, which is the same as the one on these pages. Refer to the quote on the back cover. Sunday rest can be difficult for us to observe in our modern culture. Some ways to help the Sunday rest are to celebrate family times; to visit friends, family, and the sick; to participate in cultural events and in faith formation sessions or missions.

Exercise

- Working in small groups invite the participants to do the exercise on page four which asks them to list persons who may not feel welcome at Sunday Assemblies. Suggest that they choose an action or activity that is simple, concrete, and feasible.

Take it home

- Before the end of the evening, ask the small groups to talk once more about how they plan to take home and live what they have learned. Refer to the reflections, and suggest they use them to help apply the core message of this booklet. Invite them to make concrete and realistic plans. Allow a few minutes for this discussion.

Conclusion

- Go to slide 11 and announce the time and place of the next gathering.
- Go to slide 12 and invite everyone to pray the closing prayer aloud. (You can make copies of the prayer, found on page 29 of this guide, or use the prayer of Blessed John XXIII on page 5.) You can, instead, invite the group to offer spontaneous prayer. You may also close the evening with the dismissal song on the CD.

Session Plan for Reflection Booklet **39**

What Is a Household of Faith?

Content summary

Honoring parents: the fourth commandment (based on articles 2196–2257 in the *Catechism of the Catholic Church*)

- According to the fourth commandment, God has willed that we should honor our parents and those whom he has vested with authority for our good.
- Children owe their parents respect, gratitude, just obedience, and assistance.
- Families have the first responsibility for the education of their children in the faith, prayer, and all the virtues. They have the duty to provide as much as possible for the physical and spiritual needs of their children.
- As citizens we have the duty to work with civil authority to build up society in a spirit of truth, justice, solidarity, and freedom.

Preparation

- Read through the booklet once, reflectively. Reread it and make your own notes.
- Read through the session plan and become comfortable with the format.
- For more background, read articles 2196–2257 of the *Catechism*. Mark and look up any unfamiliar words.
- Decide if and when you will do the exercise found after the material for pages six and seven. Have the materials needed.
- See pages 12–13 in this guide for other steps for preparation and materials needed.

Opening

- After introductions, if the number of participants is ten or more, ask them to form small groups. If the assembly is a large one, have each group choose a spokesperson.
- Have PowerPoint slide 1 (the cover illustration) on the screen as you begin.
- Open with the prayer found on page 4 in the introductory section of this guide. You may make copies for the participants. Or use the gathering song on the CD.
- Use the Question of the Week approach to break open the word of God from the Sunday liturgy (see 6 on page 12). Then continue with the *Growing Faith* booklet.

Pages two and three

Read and reflect

- Make sure everyone has a copy of the booklet.
- Ask the participants to read pages two and three of the booklet quietly. Tell them they will have a few minutes to do so (about five minutes).
- Invite them to mark the text when they read something that strikes them.

Share it with others

- Read the reflection on slide 2 and/or the reflection(s) provided in the booklet. Ask participants to discuss these questions in their small groups as a means of applying what they have learned in the text. Encourage them to take notes in their booklets. Give them several minutes to do all this. You may wish to play quiet music in the background during this time.
- If the assembly is large, ask the spokesperson of each small group to share a summary of the group's discussion with the larger group. Write on the board a short version or outline of all the responses.
- Use the PowerPoint slide 3 to provide the group with a visual of a Scripture passage. Open your Bibles to Exodus 20:12, and select a few verses to read aloud. How does this Scripture passage relate to what you have just read and discussed?
- Pause for a few moments of silence, then go to the illustration on slide 4, which is also found in the booklet. Ask the participants to look at the illustration. On the back cover you will find a reference for this illustration, from Scripture or the *Catechism*, that may assist you. Families share household life together. The household becomes a holy place, a real "domestic church." "The family finds in the plan of God the Creator and Redeemer not only its identity, what it is, but also its mission, what it can and should do. Since, in God's plan it has been established as an 'intimate community of life and love,' the family has the mission to become more and more what it is, in an effort that will find fulfillment in the Kingdom of God" (*The Role of the Christian Family in the Modern World*, 17).
- Invite feedback and general conversation about this illustration and its commentary (about five minutes).

Break

Pages four and five

The illustration

- Invite the participants to look at the illustration on slide 5, which is the same as the one in the booklet. Ask questions such as: What are the elements of a family meal (besides the obvious material ones)? Are you able to share at least a few meals together each week as a family? Why is that important?
- Refer to the quote on the back cover. "The Christian family is a communion of persons." The chief way to build a "household of faith" is to gather frequently for shared meals. At such gatherings we share about our lives, we come to know one another, and we meet Christ in one another. Families learn to live in harmony to fulfill duties and responsibilities, and to love and forgive one another.
- Invite feedback on this illustration and its commentary (about 5 minutes).

Read and reflect

- Ask participants to read pages four and five. Follow the same process for reading and reflection that you used for the first pages.

Share it with others

- Read the reflection on slide 6 and/or the reflection(s) provided in the booklet. Use the same format for group discussion and sharing as you did for the previous pages.
- Use PowerPoint slide 7 to provide the group with a visual of a Scripture passage. Open your Bibles to Colossians 3:20, and select a few verses to read aloud. How does this Scripture passage relate to what you have just read and discussed?
- Pause for a few moments of silence.

Pages six and seven

Personal experience

- Ask everyone to look at the heading on page six, "Civil society and the fourth commandment." Invite them to reflect on these questions: What are some positive experiences you have had as a citizen? Some negative ones? Why do civil authority and laws exist?

Read and reflect

- Again, follow the same process for reading and reflection on pages six and seven.

Share it with others

- Read the reflection on slide 8 and/or the reflection(s) provided in the booklet. Use the same format for group discussion and sharing.
- Use PowerPoint slide 9 to provide the group with a visual of a Scripture passage. Open your Bibles to Matthew 20:26, and select a few verses to read aloud. How does this Scripture passage relate to what you have just read and discussed?
- Pause for a few moments of silence, then ask the participants to look at the illustration on slide 10, which is the same as the one on these pages. Refer to the quote on the back cover. Just as we are called to honor and obey our parents, we are also enjoined by the fourth commandment to follow the directions of civil authorities and government leaders, such as the president, the mayor, judges, and the police. As citizens we should also vote, pay taxes, and support whatever is for the good of all. It's all part of how we believe God orders the human community.

Exercise

- Invite the participants to work in small groups to complete the exercise on page four which asks them to make a chart showing the makeup of your parish. If time permits, you might ask the small groups to share their charts with the entire group.

Take it home

- Before the end of the evening, ask the small groups to talk once more about how they plan to take home and live what they have learned. Refer to the reflections, and suggest they use them to help apply the core message of this booklet. Invite them to make concrete and realistic plans. Allow a few minutes for this discussion.

Conclusion

- Go to slide 11 and announce the time and place of the next gathering.
- Go to slide 12 and invite everyone to pray the closing prayer aloud. (You can make copies of the prayer, found on page 29 of this guide, or use the prayer of Blessed John XXIII on page 5.) You can, instead, invite the group to offer spontaneous prayer. You may also close the evening with the dismissal song on the CD.

Session Plan for Reflection Booklet **40**

How Do We Protect the Living?

Content summary

On the taking of life: the fifth commandment (based on articles 2258–2330 in the *Catechism of the Catholic Church*)

- Every human life, from the moment of conception until death, is sacred because the human person is created in the image and likeness of God.
- The murder of a human being is gravely contrary to the dignity of the person and the holiness of the Creator.
- We are bound to reject abortion, to protect the embryo, and to defend life in every other way. The death penalty is normally against church teaching as well.
- The arms race is one of the greatest curses on the human race. The harm it inflicts, especially on the poor, is more than can be endured.

Preparation

- Read through the booklet once, reflectively. Reread it and make your own notes.
- Read through the session plan and become comfortable with the format.
- For more background, read articles 2258–2330 of the *Catechism*. Mark and look up any unfamiliar words.
- Decide if and when you will do the exercise found after the material for pages six and seven. Have the materials needed.
- See pages 12–13 in this guide for other steps for preparation and materials needed.

Opening

- After introductions, if the number of participants is ten or more, ask them to form small groups. If the assembly is a large one, have each group choose a spokesperson.
- Have PowerPoint slide 1 (the cover illustration) on the screen as you begin.

- Open with the prayer found on page 4 in the introductory section of this guide. You may make copies for the participants. Or use the gathering song on the CD.
- Use the Question of the Week approach to break open the word of God from the Sunday liturgy (see 6 on page 12). Then continue with the *Growing Faith* booklet.

Pages two and three

Read and reflect

- Make sure everyone has a copy of the booklet.
- Ask the participants to read pages two and three of the booklet quietly. Tell them they will have a few minutes to do so (about five minutes).
- Invite them to mark the text when they read something that strikes them.

Share it with others

- Read the reflection on slide 2 and/or the reflection(s) provided in the booklet. Ask participants to discuss these questions in their small groups as a means of applying what they have learned in the text. Encourage them to take notes in their booklets. Give them several minutes to do all this. You may wish to play quiet music in the background during this time.
- If the assembly is large, ask the spokesperson of each small group to share a summary of the group's discussion with the larger group. Write on the board a short version or outline of all the responses.
- Use the PowerPoint slide 3 to provide the group with a visual of a Scripture passage. Open your Bibles to Exodus 20:13, and select a few verses to read aloud. How does this Scripture passage relate to what you have just read and discussed?
- Pause for a few moments of silence, then go to the illustration on slide 4, which is also found in the booklet. Ask the participants to look at the illustration. On the back cover you will find a reference for this illustration, from Scripture or the *Catechism,* that may assist you. There are many ways for us to defend life. One of them is to work to end capital punishment in our society. Despite their crimes prisoners are loved by God, and their conversion and amendment is always possible while they are living. Taking their lives should not be in our hands but God's.
- Invite feedback and general conversation about this illustration and its commentary (about five minutes).

Break

Pages four and five

The illustration

- Invite the participants to look at the illustration on slide 5, which is the same as the one in the booklet. Ask questions such as: Are you interested in any particular sport(s)? What are some of the advantages of taking good care of our bodies? How would you link them to the fifth commandment?
- Refer to the quote on the back cover. "Life and physical health are precious gifts." Among the ways the fifth commandment calls us to holiness is by caring for our own health, by making healthy choices regarding diet and exercise and habits such as smoking. We should also do what we can to protect the life of the unborn child, the sick, the elderly, and the mentally challenged.
- Invite feedback on this illustration and its commentary (about 5 minutes).

Read and reflect

- Ask participants to read pages four and five. Follow the same process for reading and reflection that you used for the first pages.

Share it with others

- Read the reflection on slide 6 and/or the reflection(s) provided in the booklet. Use the same format for group discussion and sharing as you did for the previous pages.
- Use PowerPoint slide 7 to provide the group with a visual of a Scripture passage. Open your Bibles to 1 Corinthians 9:25, and select a few verses to read aloud. How does this Scripture passage relate to what you have just read and discussed?
- Pause for a few moments of silence.

Pages six and seven

Personal experience

- Ask everyone to look at the heading on page seven, "Avoiding war." Invite them to reflect on these questions: Do you think war is justified under any circumstances? What makes war today different from war many years ago? What can you do to prevent war?

Read and reflect

- Again, follow the same process for reading and reflection on pages six and seven.

Share it with others

- Read the reflection on slide 8 and/or the reflection(s) provided in the booklet. Use the same format for group discussion and sharing.
- Use PowerPoint slide 9 to provide the group with a visual of a Scripture passage. Open your Bibles to Matthew 5:9, and select a few verses to read aloud. How does this Scripture passage relate to what you have just read and discussed?
- Pause for a few moments of silence, then ask the participants to look at the illustration on slide 10, which is the same as the one on these pages. Refer to the quote on the back cover. Avoiding war in our time requires that nations work together in solidarity. The United Nations provides one means for doing that, to keep channels of communication open among nations, and to avoid a headlong rush into violence and war. Each of us, in turn, is called to be a peacemaker within our own sphere, to cultivate charity and love, and work for justice.

Exercise

- After reading the booklet, discuss in small groups which types of injustice and taking of human life are practiced in your community. What can you do about it?

Take it home

- Before the end of the evening, ask the small groups to talk once more about how they plan to take home and live what they have learned. Refer to the reflections, and suggest they use them to help apply the core message of this booklet. Invite them to make concrete and realistic plans. Allow a few minutes for this discussion.

Conclusion

- Go to slide 11 and announce the time and place of the next gathering.
- Go to slide 12 and invite everyone to pray the closing prayer aloud. (You can make copies of the prayer, found on page 29 of this guide, or use the prayer of Blessed John XXIII on page 5.) You can, instead, invite the group to offer spontaneous prayer. You may also close the evening with the dismissal song on the CD.

Session Plan for Reflection Booklet **41**

How Can We Live in Love?

Content summary

Called to chastity: the sixth and ninth commandments (based on articles 2331–2400 and 2514–2533 in the *Catechism of the Catholic Church*)

- By creating the human person, man and woman, God gives each one personal dignity. Man and woman should each acknowledge and accept their sexual identity.
- Chastity means the full and complete integration of sexuality within the person.
- The covenant that spouses have freely entered into entails faithful love. It imposes on them the obligation not to break their marriage vows.
- The ninth commandment warns against lust or sexual desire outside of marriage.

Preparation

- Read through the booklet once, reflectively. Reread it and make your own notes.
- Read through the session plan and become comfortable with the format.
- For more background, read articles 2331–2400 and 2514–2533 of the *Catechism*. Mark and look up any unfamiliar words.
- Decide if and when you will do the exercise found after the material for pages six and seven. Have the materials needed.
- See pages 12–13 in this guide for other steps for preparation and materials needed.

Opening

- After introductions, if the number of participants is ten or more, ask them to form small groups. If the assembly is a large one, have each group choose a spokesperson.
- Have PowerPoint slide 1 (the cover illustration) on the screen as you begin.
- Open with the prayer found on page 4 in the introductory section of this guide. You may make copies for the participants. Or use the gathering song on the CD.
- Use the Question of the Week approach to break open the word of God from the Sunday liturgy (see 6 on page 12). Then continue with the *Growing Faith* booklet.

Pages two and three

Read and reflect

- Make sure everyone has a copy of the booklet.
- Ask the participants to read pages two and three of the booklet quietly. Tell them they will have a few minutes to do so (about five minutes).
- Invite them to mark the text when they read something that strikes them.

Share it with others

- Read the reflection on slide 2 and/or the reflection(s) provided in the booklet. Ask participants to discuss these questions in their small groups as a means of applying what they have learned in the text. Encourage them to take notes in their booklets. Give them several minutes to do all this. You may wish to play quiet music in the background during this time.
- If the assembly is large, ask the spokesperson of each small group to share a summary of the group's discussion with the larger group. Write on the board a short version or outline of all the responses.
- Use the PowerPoint slide 3 to provide the group with a visual of a Scripture passage. Open your Bibles to Genesis 1:26–28, and select a few verses to read aloud. How does this Scripture passage relate to what you have just read and discussed?
- Pause for a few moments of silence, then go to the illustration on slide 4, which is also found in the booklet. Ask the participants to look at the illustration. On the back cover you will find a reference for this illustration, from Scripture or the *Catechism*, that may assist you. God made us to love one another and to develop our sexuality. The call to chastity shows us how to do that according to the way God has created us and in the way suited to our state in life: marriage, the single life, priesthood, or religious life.
- Invite feedback and general conversation about this illustration and its commentary (about five minutes).

Break

Pages four and five

The illustration

- Invite the participants to look at the illustration on slide 5, which is the same as the one in the booklet. Ask questions such as: How would you describe the picture of the family on page five? How does it capture the theme of this booklet?
- Refer to the quote on the back cover. "A child is a gift." Children are truly a gift from God. When we receive this gift as parents or a family, we accept a vocation to join in God's own creative work.
- Invite feedback on this illustration and its commentary (about 5 minutes).

Read and reflect

- Ask participants to read pages four and five. Follow the same process for reading and reflection that you used for the first pages.

Share it with others

- Read the reflection on slide 6 and/or the reflection(s) provided in the booklet. Use the same format for group discussion and sharing as you did for the previous pages.
- Use PowerPoint slide 7 to provide the group with a visual of a Scripture passage. Open your Bibles to 2 Corinthians 7:1, and select a few verses to read aloud. How does this Scripture passage relate to what you have just read and discussed?
- Pause for a few moments of silence.

Pages six and seven

Personal experience

- Ask everyone to look at the heading on page six, "Challenges to marriage." Invite them to reflect on these questions: What are some of the challenges you experience or see to living the marriage vows in our society? What help does a family have?

Read and reflect

- Again, follow the same process for reading and reflection on pages six and seven.

Share it with others

- Read the reflection on slide 8 and/or the reflection(s) provided in the booklet. Use the same format for group discussion and sharing.

- Use PowerPoint slide 9 to provide the group with a visual of a Scripture passage. Open your Bibles to 2 Corinthians 5:17, and select a few verses to read aloud. How does this Scripture passage relate to what you have just read and discussed?

- Pause for a few moments of silence, then ask the participants to look at the illustration on slide 10, which is the same as the one on these pages. Refer to the quote on the back cover. Our friendships, except with our spouse, do not involve sexual activity. Indeed, except for the person to whom we are married, we are to be "celibate" in our relationships and cultivate purity of heart and modesty in our thoughts, words, and actions. Chastity enriches our friendships and raises them to a higher level.

Exercise

- The exercise on page four asks the participants to make a list of affirmations they could offer family, friends, and others. Invite them to complete this activity.

Take it home

- Before the end of the evening, ask the small groups to talk once more about how they plan to take home and live what they have learned. Refer to the reflections, and suggest they use them to help apply the core message of this booklet. Invite them to make concrete and realistic plans. Allow a few minutes for this discussion.

Conclusion

- Go to slide 11 and announce the time and place of the next gathering.

- Go to slide 12 and invite everyone to pray the closing prayer aloud. (You can make copies of the prayer, found on page 29 of this guide, or use the prayer of Blessed John XXIII on page 5.) You can, instead, invite the group to offer spontaneous prayer. You may also close the evening with the dismissal song on the CD.

Session Plan for Reflection Booklet **42**

When Do We Have Too Much?

Content summary

Possessions, greed, and generosity: the seventh and tenth commandments (based on articles 2401–2463 and 2534–2557 in the *Catechism of the Catholic Church*)

- The seventh commandment calls us to the practice of justice and charity in handling and managing earthly goods and the fruits of our labor.
- The goods of creation are destined for the entire human race. The right to private property does not take away rights of all people to share in the goods of the earth.
- The dominion the Creator has given us over the mineral, vegetable, and animal resources of the universe must include respect for our moral obligations, including our obligations toward generations to come.
- The tenth commandment forbids avarice arising from a passion for riches and the power they bestow.

Preparation

- Read through the booklet once, reflectively. Reread it and make your own notes.
- Read through the session plan and become comfortable with the format.
- For more background, read articles 2401–2463 and 2534–2557 of the *Catechism*. Mark and look up any unfamiliar words.
- Decide if and when you will do the exercise found after the material for pages six and seven. Have the materials needed.
- See pages 12–13 in this guide for other steps for preparation and materials needed.

Opening

- After introductions, if the number of participants is ten or more, ask them to form small groups. If the assembly is a large one, have each group choose a spokesperson.
- Have PowerPoint slide 1 (the cover illustration) on the screen as you begin.

- Open with the prayer found on page 4 in the introductory section of this guide. You may make copies for the participants. Or use the gathering song on the CD.
- Use the Question of the Week approach to break open the word of God from the Sunday liturgy (see 6 on page 12). Then continue with the *Growing Faith* booklet.

Pages two and three

Read and reflect

- Make sure everyone has a copy of the booklet.
- Ask the participants to read pages two and three of the booklet quietly. Tell them they will have a few minutes to do so (about five minutes).
- Invite them to mark the text when they read something that strikes them.

Share it with others

- Read the reflection on slide 2 and/or the reflection(s) provided in the booklet. Ask participants to discuss these questions in their small groups as a means of applying what they have learned in the text. Encourage them to take notes in their booklets. Give them several minutes to do all this. You may wish to play quiet music in the background during this time.
- If the assembly is large, ask the spokesperson of each small group to share a summary of the group's discussion with the larger group. Write on the board a short version or outline of all the responses.
- Use the PowerPoint slide 3 to provide the group with a visual of a Scripture passage. Open your Bibles to Matthew 5:42, and select a few verses to read aloud. How does this Scripture passage relate to what you have just read and discussed?
- Pause for a few moments of silence, then go to the illustration on slide 4, which is also found in the booklet. Ask the participants to look at the illustration. On the back cover you will find a reference for this illustration, from Scripture or the *Catechism*, that may assist you. We humans imitate Christ when we reach the point of saying, "Enough is enough." Most of us in the first world are already so well off that we have more than our own share of the world's resources. Like the abundance pictured on page two, our tables are overflowing. We need to be generous in sharing, and to avoid any form of stealing, including excessive spending and waste, evading tax payments, and failing to pay just debts.
- Invite feedback and general conversation about this illustration and its commentary (about five minutes).

Break

Pages four and five

The illustration

- Invite the participants to look at the illustration on slide 5, which is the same as the one in the booklet. Ask questions such as: Do you have a pet or farm animals? How do you treat them? Do you support any animal protection groups?
- Refer to the quote on the back cover. "God entrusted animals to our stewardship." We are responsible for the care of any pets or livestock we have. Animals provide us with companionship and food and should not be abused, tortured, or killed inhumanely. However, we must not lavish on them the love or attention reserved only for human persons.
- Invite feedback on this illustration and its commentary (about 5 minutes).

Read and reflect

- Ask participants to read pages four and five. Follow the same process for reading and reflection that you used for the first pages.

Share it with others

- Read the reflection on slide 6 and/or the reflection(s) provided in the booklet. Use the same format for group discussion and sharing as you did for the previous pages.
- Use PowerPoint slide 7 to provide the group with a visual of a Scripture passage. Open your Bibles to Luke 6:20, and select a few verses to read aloud. How does this Scripture passage relate to what you have just read and discussed?
- Pause for a few moments of silence.

Pages six and seven

Personal experience

- Ask everyone to look at the heading on page six, "Loving the poor." Invite them to reflect on these questions: What does "loving the poor" mean to you in practical terms? If a poor person were to approach you on the street, how would you react? What would you do?

Read and reflect

• Again, follow the same process for reading and reflection on pages six and seven.

Share it with others

• Read the reflection on slide 8 and/or the reflection(s) provided in the booklet. Use the same format for group discussion and sharing.

• Use PowerPoint slide 9 to provide the group with a visual of a Scripture passage. Open your Bibles to Luke 6:27–28, and select a few verses to read aloud. How does this Scripture passage relate to what you have just read and discussed?

• Pause for a few moments of silence, then ask the participants to look at the illustration on slide 10, which is the same as the one on these pages. Refer to the quote on the back cover. Jesus asks us to love and care for the least among us. Like St. Katharine Drexel, we should put our money, energy, and time to work helping others. Life is short, and this is our only chance to serve our sisters and brothers. The words of mercy are a guide for us in practicing concrete love. "I was hungry and you gave me food, I was thirsty and you gave me drink" (Matthew 25:35).

Exercise

• Invite the participants to look up some Scripture passages, especially in the New Testament, that address the topics of greed and generosity, stealing, or caring for the earth's resources.

Take it home

• Before the end of the evening, ask the small groups to talk once more about how they plan to take home and live what they have learned. Refer to the reflections, and suggest they use them to help apply the core message of this booklet. Invite them to make concrete and realistic plans. Allow a few minutes for this discussion.

Conclusion

• Go to slide 11 and announce the time and place of the next gathering.

• Go to slide 12 and invite everyone to pray the closing prayer aloud. (You can make copies of the prayer, found on page 29 of this guide, or use the prayer of Blessed John XXIII on page 5.) You can, instead, invite the group to offer spontaneous prayer. You may also close the evening with the dismissal song on the CD.

Session Plan for Reflection Booklet **43**

How Do We Tell the Truth?

Content summary

Truth: the eighth commandment (based on articles 2464–2513 in the *Catechism of the Catholic Church*)

- Honesty consists in being truthful in deeds and in words.
- Respect for the reputation and honor of other persons forbids all gossip and speaking badly of others, even when a statement is true.
- Lying consists in saying what is false with the intention of deceiving our neighbor.
- The sacramental seal is inviolable. Professional secrets must be kept. Confidences prejudicial to another are not to be divulged.

Preparation

- Read through the booklet once, reflectively. Reread it and make your own notes.
- Read through the session plan and become comfortable with the format.
- For more background, read articles 2464–2513 of the *Catechism*. Mark and look up any unfamiliar words.
- Decide if and when you will do the exercise found after the material for pages six and seven. Have the materials needed.
- See pages 12–13 in this guide for other steps for preparation and materials needed.

Opening

- After introductions, if the number of participants is ten or more, ask them to form small groups. If the assembly is a large one, have each group choose a spokesperson.
- Have PowerPoint slide 1 (the cover illustration) on the screen as you begin.
- Open with the prayer found on page 4 in the introductory section of this guide. You may make copies for the participants. Or use the gathering song on the CD.
- Use the Question of the Week approach to break open the word of God from the Sunday liturgy (see 6 on page 12). Then continue with the *Growing Faith* booklet.

Pages two and three

Read and reflect

- Make sure everyone has a copy of the booklet.
- Ask the participants to read pages two and three of the booklet quietly. Tell them they will have a few minutes to do so (about five minutes).
- Invite them to mark the text when they read something that strikes them.

Share it with others

- Read the reflection on slide 2 and/or the reflection(s) provided in the booklet. Ask participants to discuss these questions in their small groups as a means of applying what they have learned in the text. Encourage them to take notes in their booklets. Give them several minutes to do all this. You may wish to play quiet music in the background during this time.
- If the assembly is large, ask the spokesperson of each small group to share a summary of the group's discussion with the larger group. Write on the board a short version or outline of all the responses.
- Use the PowerPoint slide 3 to provide the group with a visual of a Scripture passage. Open your Bibles to John 1:14, and select a few verses to read aloud. How does this Scripture passage relate to what you have just read and discussed?
- Pause for a few moments of silence, then go to the illustration on slide 4, which is also found in the booklet. Ask the participants to look at the illustration. On the back cover you will find a reference for this illustration, from Scripture or the *Catechism*, that may assist you. Swearing to tell the truth in courts of law is the basis for living in a well-ordered society. Believing that the truth can be known and that people can be judged fairly creates trust in our courts. We also give witness to the importance of truth in other ways, as did the early Christians who accepted death, rather than lie about their faith.
- Invite feedback and general conversation about this illustration and its commentary (about five minutes).

Break

Pages four and five

The illustration

- Invite the participants to look at the illustration on slide 5, which is the same as the one in the booklet. Ask questions such as: What might these young people be talking about? Do you have friends with whom you share secrets? How would you feel if one of them lied to you, or betrayed your secret?
- Refer to the quote on the back cover. "We could not live with one another [without] being truthful." Society depends upon our being honest with each other. Nowhere is this more true than in friendship. Like these two people we must tell each other the truth.
- Invite feedback on this illustration and its commentary (about 5 minutes).

Read and reflect

- Ask participants to read pages four and five. Follow the same process for reading and reflection that you used for the first pages.

Share it with others

- Read the reflection on slide 6 and/or the reflection(s) provided in the booklet. Use the same format for group discussion and sharing as you did for the previous pages.
- Use PowerPoint slide 7 to provide the group with a visual of a Scripture passage. Open your Bibles to 1 John 1:6, and select a few verses to read aloud. How does this Scripture passage relate to what you have just read and discussed?
- Pause for a few moments of silence.

Pages six and seven

Personal experience

- Ask everyone to look at the heading on page six, "The media." Invite them to reflect on these questions: Do you accept everything the media presents at "face value"? While often providing a valuable service, how can the media sometimes distort the truth? How has it affected you and your family?

Read and reflect
- Again, follow the same process for reading and reflection on pages six and seven.

Share it with others
- Read the reflection on slide 8 and/or the reflection(s) provided in the booklet. Use the same format for group discussion and sharing.
- Use PowerPoint slide 9 to provide the group with a visual of a Scripture passage. Open your Bibles to John 18:37, and select a few verses to read aloud. How does this Scripture passage relate to what you have just read and discussed?
- Pause for a few moments of silence, then ask the participants to look at the illustration on slide 10, which is the same as the one on these pages. Refer to the quote on the back cover. Having the truth available to the general public is something we may take for granted. Even in the best societies today, however, the truth is often manipulated and twisted to gain political or financial advantage. Public truth telling is essential! This includes not only news reporting, but programs for entertainment and advertising.

Exercise
- Invite the participants to do the exercise on page four, which asks them to write a short prayer asking God for the courage to live by what they believe.

Take it home
- Before the end of the evening, ask the small groups to talk once more about how they plan to take home and live what they have learned. Refer to the reflections, and suggest they use them to help apply the core message of this booklet. Invite them to make concrete and realistic plans. Allow a few minutes for this discussion.

Conclusion
- Go to slide 11 and announce the time and place of the next gathering.
- Go to slide 12 and invite everyone to pray the closing prayer aloud. (You can make copies of the prayer, found on page 29 of this guide, or use the prayer of Blessed John XXIII on page 5.) You can, instead, invite the group to offer spontaneous prayer. You may also close the evening with the dismissal song on the CD.

Session Plan for Reflection Booklet **44**

What Is Prayer?

Content summary

We are called to an encounter with God (based on articles 2558–2597 in the *Catechism of the Catholic Church*)

- In prayer, the Holy Spirit raises our minds and hearts to God.
- Prayer is the privileged moment of intimacy with God where we discuss our lives, the needs of the world, and the ways our hearts move within us.
- God calls each person to this mysterious encounter with himself.
- Prayer unfolds throughout the whole history of salvation as a reciprocal call between God and us.

Preparation

- Read through the booklet once, reflectively. Reread it and make your own notes.
- Read through the session plan and become comfortable with the format.
- For more background, read articles 2558–2597 of the *Catechism*. Mark and look up any unfamiliar words.
- Decide if and when you will do the exercise found after the material for pages six and seven. Have the materials needed.
- See pages 12–13 in this guide for other steps for preparation and materials needed.

Opening

- After introductions, if the number of participants is ten or more, ask them to form small groups. If the assembly is a large one, have each group choose a spokesperson.
- Have PowerPoint slide 1 (the cover illustration) on the screen as you begin.
- Open with the prayer found on page 4 in the introductory section of this guide. You may make copies for the participants. Or use the gathering song on the CD.
- Use the Question of the Week approach to break open the word of God from the Sunday liturgy (see 6 on page 12). Then continue with the *Growing Faith* booklet.

Pages two and three

Read and reflect

- Make sure everyone has a copy of the booklet.
- Ask the participants to read pages two and three of the booklet quietly. Tell them they will have a few minutes to do so (about five minutes).
- Invite them to mark the text when they read something that strikes them.

Share it with others

- Read the reflection on slide 2 and/or the reflection(s) provided in the booklet. Ask participants to discuss these questions in their small groups as a means of applying what they have learned in the text. Encourage them to take notes in their booklets. Give them several minutes to do all this. You may wish to play quiet music in the background during this time.
- If the assembly is large, ask the spokesperson of each small group to share a summary of the group's discussion with the larger group. Write on the board a short version or outline of all the responses.
- Use the PowerPoint slide 3 to provide the group with a visual of a Scripture passage. Open your Bibles to Luke 11:28, and select a few verses to read aloud. How does this Scripture passage relate to what you have just read and discussed?
- Pause for a few moments of silence, then go to the illustration on slide 4, which is also found in the booklet. Ask the participants to look at the illustration. On the back cover you will find a reference for this illustration, from Scripture or the *Catechism*, that may assist you. The Holy Spirit causes prayer to surge within us, just as it did for St. Thérèse of Lisieux. However, we need to open up the time and space within our hearts for this to happen. How and when can we make more time for prayer?
- Invite feedback and general conversation about this illustration and its commentary (about five minutes).

Break

Pages four and five

The illustration

- Invite the participants to look at the illustration on slide 5, which is the same as the one in the booklet. This is a picture of the prophet Elijah. Where do you think he is going? How can he be a symbol for our prayer?
- Refer to the quote on the back cover. "The mysterious presence of God." Elijah went to hear God's voice and did not find it in the earthquake, the fire, or the great wind. Only in the sound of sheer silence did Elijah finally recognize the voice of God. We, too, need silence to listen to and recognize God's voice in our lives.
- Invite feedback on this illustration and its commentary (about 5 minutes).

Read and reflect

- Ask participants to read pages four and five. Follow the same process for reading and reflection that you used for the first pages.

Share it with others

- Read the reflection on slide 6 and/or the reflection(s) provided in the booklet. Use the same format for group discussion and sharing as you did for the previous pages.
- Use PowerPoint slide 7 to provide the group with a visual of a Scripture passage. Open your Bibles 1 Kings 19:11–12, and select a few verses to read aloud. How does this Scripture passage relate to what you have just read and discussed?
- Pause for a few moments of silence.

Pages six and seven

Personal experience

- Ask everyone to look at the heading on page six, "I believe in music." Invite them to reflect on these questions: How does music affect you? What part does it play in your worship?

Read and reflect

- Again, follow the same process for reading and reflection on pages six and seven.

Share it with others

- Read the reflection on slide 8 and/or the reflection(s) provided in the booklet. Use the same format for group discussion and sharing.

- Use PowerPoint slide 9 to provide the group with a visual of a Scripture passage. Open your Bibles to 2 Samuel 7:18, and select a few verses to read aloud. How does this Scripture passage relate to what you have just read and discussed?

- Pause for a few moments of silence, then ask the participants to look at the illustration on slide 10, which is the same as the one on these pages. Refer to the quote on the back cover. David did not write all the psalms, but he is the icon of this form of prayer. The psalms have an important place in Christian prayer. They are used after the First Reading in the Liturgy of the Word at Mass, and are a major part of the Liturgy of the Hours. They can inspire our personal prayer, since they include all the forms of prayer.

Exercise

- Participants can do the exercise on page six, which invites them to write a psalm of their own.

Take it home

- Before the end of the evening, ask the small groups to talk once more about how they plan to take home and live what they have learned. Refer to the reflections, and suggest they use them to help apply the core message of this booklet. Invite them to make concrete and realistic plans. Allow a few minutes for this discussion.

Conclusion

- Go to slide 11 and announce the time and place of the next gathering.

- Go to slide 12 and invite everyone to pray the closing prayer aloud. (You can make copies of the prayer, found on page 29 of this guide, or use the prayer of Blessed John XXIII on page 5.) You can, instead, invite the group to offer spontaneous prayer. You may also close the evening with the dismissal song on the CD.

Session Plan for Reflection Booklet **45**

How Do We Pray?

Content summary

Forms of prayer (based on articles 2598–2649 in the *Catechism of the Catholic Church*)

- The Holy Spirit, who teaches the Church and helps us remember all that Jesus said also instructs us in the life of prayer.
- The basic forms of prayer are blessing, petition, intercession, thanksgiving, and praise.
- The gospels provide an image of Jesus as constantly prayerful.
- Because God blesses the human heart, we can in return bless God who is the source of every blessing.

Preparation

- Read through the booklet once, reflectively. Reread it and make your own notes.
- Read through the session plan and become comfortable with the format.
- For more background, read articles 2598–2649 of the *Catechism*. Mark and look up any unfamiliar words.
- Decide if and when you will do the exercise found after the material for pages six and seven. Have the materials needed.
- See pages 12–13 in this guide for other steps for preparation and materials needed.

Opening

- After introductions, if the number of participants is ten or more, ask them to form small groups. If the assembly is a large one, have each group choose a spokesperson.
- Have PowerPoint slide 1 (the cover illustration) on the screen as you begin.
- Open with the prayer found on page 4 in the introductory section of this guide. You may make copies for the participants. Or use the gathering song on the CD.
- Use the Question of the Week approach to break open the word of God from the Sunday liturgy (see 6 on page 12). Then continue with the *Growing Faith* booklet.

Pages two and three

Read and reflect

- Make sure everyone has a copy of the booklet.
- Ask the participants to read pages two and three of the booklet quietly. Tell them they will have a few minutes to do so (about five minutes).
- Invite them to mark the text when they read something that strikes them.

Share it with others

- Read the reflection on slide 2 and/or the reflection(s) provided in the booklet. Ask participants to discuss these questions in their small groups as a means of applying what they have learned in the text. Encourage them to take notes in their booklets. Give them several minutes to do all this. You may wish to play quiet music in the background during this time.
- If the assembly is large, ask the spokesperson of each small group to share a summary of the group's discussion with the larger group. Write on the board a short version or outline of all the responses.
- Use the PowerPoint slide 3 to provide the group with a visual of a Scripture passage. Open your Bibles to Luke 1:46–47, and select a few verses to read aloud. How does this Scripture passage relate to what you have just read and discussed?
- Pause for a few moments of silence, then go to the illustration on slide 4, which is also found in the booklet. Ask the participants to look at the illustration. On the back cover you will find a reference for this illustration, from Scripture or the *Catechism*, that may assist you. Mary is a wonderful model of prayerfulness for us. She trusted that whatever happened, God's promises would never be violated. God would be with her always; she was wholly God's because God was wholly her.
- Invite feedback and general conversation about this illustration and its commentary (about five minutes).

Break

Pages four and five

The illustration

- Invite the participants to look at the illustration on slide 5, which is the same as the one in the booklet. Ask questions such as: Is Jesus a model of prayer for you? How and why?

- Refer to the quote on the back cover. "Jesus often draws apart to pray." Jesus often went off to lonely places to pray alone, but never more so than in this garden. Like him we should turn to God in times of great need, trusting that God will guide us on the right path.

- Invite feedback on this illustration and its commentary (about 5 minutes).

Read and reflect

- Ask participants to read pages four and five. Follow the same process for reading and reflection that you used for the first pages.

Share it with others

- Read the reflection on slide 6 and/or the reflection(s) provided in the booklet. Use the same format for group discussion and sharing as you did for the previous pages.

- Use PowerPoint slide 7 to provide the group with a visual of a Scripture passage. Open your Bibles to Luke 22:41, and select a few verses to read aloud. How does this Scripture passage relate to what you have just read and discussed?

- Pause for a few moments of silence.

Pages six and seven

Personal experience

- Ask everyone to look at the heading on page six, "Forms of prayer." Invite them to reflect on these questions: What motivates most of your prayer? Do you pray because you need something, or to thank God, to bless or praise God, to pray for others?

Read and reflect

- Again, follow the same process for reading and reflection on pages six and seven.

Share it with others

- Read the reflection on slide 8 and/or the reflection(s) provided in the booklet. Use the same format for group discussion and sharing.
- Use PowerPoint slide 9 to provide the group with a visual of a Scripture passage. Open your Bibles to Luke 11:19, and select a few verses to read aloud. How does this Scripture passage relate to what you have just read and discussed?
- Pause for a few moments of silence, then ask the participants to look at the illustration on slide 10, which is the same as the one on these pages. Refer to the quote on the back cover. Jesus teaches us that if we ask with faith, God will provide. Learning to pray in this way creates within us deep happiness because it answers that inborn longing for God that we all have. This longing moves us to bless and praise God, to thank God for all the gifts God gives, to intercede for the good of others, and to ask for what we need to grow in health of body and spirit.

Exercise

- Invite the participants, working in small groups, to do a simple "prayer dance" by adding gestures to Mary's Magnificat (Luke 1:46–53).

Take it home

- Before the end of the evening, ask the small groups to talk once more about how they plan to take home and live what they have learned. Refer to the reflections, and suggest they use them to help apply the core message of this booklet. Invite them to make concrete and realistic plans. Allow a few minutes for this discussion.

Conclusion

- Go to slide 11 and announce the time and place of the next gathering.
- Go to slide 12 and invite everyone to pray the closing prayer aloud. (You can make copies of the prayer, found on page 29 of this guide, or use the prayer of Blessed John XXIII on page 5.) You can, instead, invite the group to offer spontaneous prayer. You may also close the evening with the dismissal song on the CD.

Session Plan for Reflection Booklet **46**

How Does God Speak to Us in Prayer?

Content summary

The wellsprings of prayer (based on articles 2650–2696 in the *Catechism of the Catholic Church*)

- The Holy Spirit in the church teaches us to pray as the children of God.
- The word of God, the liturgy of the church, and the virtues of faith, hope, and charity are sources of prayer.
- The different schools of Christian spirituality share in the living tradition of prayer and are precious guides for the spiritual life.
- The Christian family is the first place for education in prayer.

Preparation

- Read through the booklet once, reflectively. Reread it and make your own notes.
- Read through the session plan and become comfortable with the format.
- For more background, read articles 2650–2696 of the *Catechism*. Mark and look up any unfamiliar words.
- Decide if and when you will do the exercise found after the material for pages six and seven. Have the materials needed.
- See pages 12–13 in this guide for other steps for preparation and materials needed.

Opening

- After introductions, if the number of participants is ten or more, ask them to form small groups. If the assembly is a large one, have each group choose a spokesperson.
- Have PowerPoint slide 1 (the cover illustration) on the screen as you begin.
- Open with the prayer found on page 4 in the introductory section of this guide. You may make copies for the participants. Or use the gathering song on the CD.
- Use the Question of the Week approach to break open the word of God from the Sunday liturgy (see 6 on page 12). Then continue with the *Growing Faith* booklet.

Pages two and three

Read and reflect

- Make sure everyone has a copy of the booklet.
- Ask the participants to read pages two and three of the booklet quietly. Tell them they will have a few minutes to do so (about five minutes).
- Invite them to mark the text when they read something that strikes them.

Share it with others

- Read the reflection on slide 2 and/or the reflection(s) provided in the booklet. Ask participants to discuss these questions in their small groups as a means of applying what they have learned in the text. Encourage them to take notes in their booklets. Give them several minutes to do all this. You may wish to play quiet music in the background during this time.
- If the assembly is large, ask the spokesperson of each small group to share a summary of the group's discussion with the larger group. Write on the board a short version or outline of all the responses.
- Use the PowerPoint slide 3 to provide the group with a visual of a Scripture passage. Open your Bibles to Psalm 95:7–8, and select a few verses to read aloud. How does this Scripture passage relate to what you have just read and discussed?
- Pause for a few moments of silence, then go to the illustration on slide 4, which is also found in the booklet. Ask the participants to look at the illustration. On the back cover you will find a reference for this illustration, from Scripture or the *Catechism*, that may assist you. We can pray while doing the most humble tasks: folding laundry, driving the car, washing dishes, walking in a quiet place. St. Benedict taught his monks to pray while working: "ora et labora." This is good advice.
- Invite feedback and general conversation about this illustration and its commentary (about five minutes).

Break

Pages four and five

The illustration

- Invite the participants to look at the illustration on slide 5, which is the same as the one in the booklet. Ask questions such as: Have you ever made a retreat? If yes, what was it like? How can you make time for a retreat?
- Refer to the quote on the back cover. "To provide necessary solitude for prayer." Making a retreat now and then is an excellent way to enrich and enliven our faith. Retreats can be made at retreat or prayer houses, monasteries, or even at home. In fact, the way of prayer of Christians through the centuries has been influenced by the saints, who founded various religious communities and monasteries. Each person needs to find the way of prayer that best helps them grow closer to God.
- Invite feedback on this illustration and its commentary (about 5 minutes).

Read and reflect

- Ask participants to read pages four and five. Follow the same process for reading and reflection that you used for the first pages.

Share it with others

- Read the reflection on slide 6 and/or the reflection(s) provided in the booklet. Use the same format for group discussion and sharing as you did for the previous pages.
- Use PowerPoint slide 7 to provide the group with a visual of a Scripture passage. Open your Bibles to Matthew 6:6, and select a few verses to read aloud. How does this Scripture passage relate to what you have just read and discussed?
- Pause for a few moments of silence.

Pages six and seven

Personal experience

- Ask everyone to look at the heading on page six, "Guides to prayer." Invite them to reflect on these questions: What or who has been most helpful to you in developing your prayer life? Explain.

Read and reflect

- Again, follow the same process for reading and reflection on pages six and seven.

Share it with others

- Read the reflection on slide 8 and/or the reflection(s) provided in the booklet. Use the same format for group discussion and sharing.
- Use PowerPoint slide 9 to provide the group with a visual of a Scripture passage. Open your Bibles to Luke 8:15, and select a few verses to read aloud. How does this Scripture passage relate to what you have just read and discussed?
- Pause for a few moments of silence, then ask the participants to look at the illustration on slide 10, which is the same as the one on these pages. Refer to the quote on the back cover. We need to pay attention to how and when we pray, in order to have a regular prayer life. Setting aside time to be alone with God is essential. The Holy Spirit is our guide and fills our whole being. However, we also learn from one another how to pray and how to share prayer.

Exercise

- Invite the participants to complete the chart in the exercise on page six. The chart is for planning the coming "week of prayer."

Take it home

- Before the end of the evening, ask the small groups to talk once more about how they plan to take home and live what they have learned. Refer to the reflections, and suggest they use them to help apply the core message of this booklet. Invite them to make concrete and realistic plans. Allow a few minutes for this discussion.

Conclusion

- Go to slide 11 and announce the time and place of the next gathering.
- Go to slide 12 and invite everyone to pray the closing prayer aloud. (You can make copies of the prayer, found on page 29 of this guide, or use the prayer of Blessed John XXIII on page 5.) You can, instead, invite the group to offer spontaneous prayer. You may also close the evening with the dismissal song on the CD.

Session Plan for Reflection Booklet **47**

How Do We Become Persons of Prayer?

Content summary

Ways to pray and obstacles to prayer (based on articles 2697–2758 in the *Catechism of the Catholic Church*)

- The church invites us to regular prayer: daily prayers, the Liturgy of the Hours, Sunday Eucharist, and the feasts of the liturgical year.
- The Christian tradition comprises three major expressions of the life of prayer: vocal prayer, meditation, and contemplative prayer. They have in common the recollection of our hearts.
- The principal difficulties in the practice of prayer are distraction and dryness.
- We can always pray; prayer is a vital necessity. Prayer and Christian life are inseparable.

Preparation

- Read through the booklet once, reflectively. Reread it and make your own notes.
- Read through the session plan and become comfortable with the format.
- For more background, read articles 2697–2758 of the *Catechism*. Mark and look up any unfamiliar words.
- Decide if and when you will do the exercise found after the material for pages six and seven. Have the materials needed.
- See pages 12–13 in this guide for other steps for preparation and materials needed.

Opening

- After introductions, if the number of participants is ten or more, ask them to form small groups. If the assembly is a large one, have each group choose a spokesperson.
- Have PowerPoint slide 1 (the cover illustration) on the screen as you begin.
- Open with the prayer found on page 4 in the introductory section of this guide. You may make copies for the participants. Or use the gathering song on the CD.

- Use the Question of the Week approach to break open the word of God from the Sunday liturgy (see 6 on page 12). Then continue with the *Growing Faith* booklet.

Pages two and three

Read and reflect

- Make sure everyone has a copy of the booklet.
- Ask the participants to read pages two and three of the booklet quietly. Tell them they will have a few minutes to do so (about five minutes).
- Invite them to mark the text when they read something that strikes them.

Share it with others

- Read the reflection on slide 2 and/or the reflection(s) provided in the booklet. Ask participants to discuss these questions in their small groups as a means of applying what they have learned in the text. Encourage them to take notes in their booklets. Give them several minutes to do all this. You may wish to play quiet music in the background during this time.
- If the assembly is large, ask the spokesperson of each small group to share a summary of the group's discussion with the larger group. Write on the board a short version or outline of all the responses.
- Use the PowerPoint slide 3 to provide the group with a visual of a Scripture passage. Open your Bibles to Matthew 15:25, and select a few verses to read aloud. How does this Scripture passage relate to what you have just read and discussed?
- Pause for a few moments of silence, then go to the illustration on slide 4, which is also found in the booklet. Ask the participants to look at the illustration. On the back cover you will find a reference for this illustration, from Scripture or the *Catechism*, that may assist you. Meditation is often accompanied by spiritual reading, reflection on nature, or listening to sacred music. Thinking about matters of faith and the church leads to important insights that might otherwise escape us. The mysteries of faith become our own, our hearts are uplifted, and we are united with Jesus.
- Invite feedback and general conversation about this illustration and its commentary (about five minutes).

Break

Pages four and five

The illustration

- Invite the participants to look at the illustration on slide 5, which is the same as the one in the booklet. Ask questions such as: What might the man in the picture be looking at? Have you ever looked out the window at the beauty of nature, or to watch your children playing?

- Refer to the quote on the back cover. "Contemplation is a gaze of faith." Contemplative prayer is the most joyous form. In contemplative prayer we simply place ourselves in the presence of God, and let God reach our hearts with solace and comfort. Inevitably such prayer leads to action! However, such prayer is not easy to attain. Prayer is a gift, and at times we may experience distractions or dryness. Here we need to turn to Christ with faith.

- Invite feedback on this illustration and its commentary (about 5 minutes).

Read and reflect

- Ask participants to read pages four and five. Follow the same process for reading and reflection that you used for the first pages.

Share it with others

- Read the reflection on slide 6 and/or the reflection(s) provided in the booklet. Use the same format for group discussion and sharing as you did for the previous pages.

- Use PowerPoint slide 7 to provide the group with a visual of a Scripture passage. Open your Bibles to Matthew 6:7, and select a few verses to read aloud. How does this Scripture passage relate to what you have just read and discussed?

- Pause for a few moments of silence.

Pages six and seven

Personal experience

- Ask everyone to look at the heading on page seven, "Perseverance in prayer." Invite them to reflect on these questions: Have you ever been tempted to "give up" on prayer? When and why? What did you do?

Read and reflect

- Again, follow the same process for reading and reflection on pages six and seven.

Share it with others

- Read the reflection on slide 8 and/or the reflection(s) provided in the booklet. Use the same format for group discussion and sharing.
- Use PowerPoint slide 9 to provide the group with a visual of a Scripture passage. Open your Bibles to Psalm 131:2, and select a few verses to read aloud. How does this Scripture passage relate to what you have just read and discussed?
- Pause for a few moments of silence, then ask the participants to look at the illustration on slide 10, which is the same as the one on these pages. Refer to the quote on the back cover. Sharing prayer with others at meal times, morning or evening prayer, or other times, is an important way to pray. Having others share in our own prayer life helps us be more faithful at prayer ourselves. We need to believe that God always hears and answers our prayer, but also be open to God's will for our good.

Exercise

- Invite participants to draw a symbol or image that represents prayer to them.

Take it home

- Before the end of the evening, ask the small groups to talk once more about how they plan to take home and live what they have learned. Refer to the reflections, and suggest they use them to help apply the core message of this booklet. Invite them to make concrete and realistic plans. Allow a few minutes for this discussion.

Conclusion

- Go to slide 11 and announce the time and place of the next gathering.
- Go to slide 12 and invite everyone to pray the closing prayer aloud. (You can make copies of the prayer, found on page 29 of this guide, or use the prayer of Blessed John XXIII on page 5.) You can, instead, invite the group to offer spontaneous prayer. You may also close the evening with the dismissal song on the CD.

Session Plan for Reflection Booklet **48**

What Is the Lord's Prayer?

Content summary for this Reflection Booklet

Praying as Jesus taught (based on articles 2759–2865 in the *Catechism of the Catholic Church*)

- The Lord's Prayer is truly the summary of the whole gospel.
- The Lord's Prayer is the basic prayer of the Christian life.
- Praying to our Father should help us want to become like God and foster in us a humble and trusting heart.
- In the Our Father, the object of the first three petitions is the glory of the Father: the sanctification of his name, the coming of the kingdom, and the fulfillment of his will. The other four petitions present our wants to God. They ask that our lives be nourished, healed of sin, and made victorious in the struggle of good over evil.

Preparation

- Read through the booklet once, reflectively. Reread it and make your own notes.
- Read through the session plan and become comfortable with the format.
- For more background, read articles 2759–2865 of the *Catechism*. Mark and look up any unfamiliar words.
- Decide if and when you will do the exercise found after the material for pages six and seven. Have the materials needed.
- See pages 12–13 in this guide for other steps for preparation and materials needed.

Opening

- After introductions, if the number of participants is ten or more, ask them to form small groups. If the assembly is a large one, have each group choose a spokesperson.
- Have PowerPoint slide 1 (the cover illustration) on the screen as you begin.
- Open with the prayer found on page 4 in the introductory section of this guide. You may make copies for the participants. Or use the gathering song on the CD.
- Use the Question of the Week approach to break open the word of God from the Sunday liturgy (see 6 on page 12). Then continue with the *Growing Faith* booklet.

Pages two and three

Read and reflect

- Make sure everyone has a copy of the booklet.
- Ask the participants to read pages two and three of the booklet quietly. Tell them they will have a few minutes to do so (about five minutes).
- Invite them to mark the text when they read something that strikes them.

Share it with others

- Read the reflection on slide 2 and/or the reflection(s) provided in the booklet. Ask participants to discuss these questions in their small groups as a means of applying what they have learned in the text. Encourage them to take notes in their booklets. Give them several minutes to do all this. You may wish to play quiet music in the background during this time.
- If the assembly is large, ask the spokesperson of each small group to share a summary of the group's discussion with the larger group. Write on the board a short version or outline of all the responses.
- Use the PowerPoint slide 3 to provide the group with a visual of a Scripture passage. Open your Bibles to Matthew 6:9–10, and select a few verses to read aloud. How does this Scripture passage relate to what you have just read and discussed?
- Pause for a few moments of silence, then go to the illustration on slide 4, which is also found in the booklet. Ask the participants to look at the illustration. On the back cover you will find a reference for this illustration, from Scripture or the *Catechism*, that may assist you. The dome of St. Peter's Basilica in Rome is a symbol of our unity as Christians. This unity is the prayer of Christ and the goal of the church. It comes about when we indeed forgive others as we want to be forgiven ourselves. Let us pray this unity may come about in our lifetime!
- Invite feedback and general conversation about this illustration and its commentary (about five minutes).

Break

Pages four and five

The illustration

- Invite the participants to look at the illustration on slide 5, which is the same as the one in the booklet. Ask questions such as: What does this picture bring to mind? Does your prayer extend to people around the world, or only your own small world?
- Refer to the quote on the back cover. "Thy will be done on earth as in heaven." God sends love and peace through us into this world. God's will is that we live in harmony, in solidarity with one another, and in balance with the earth. We also pray that God's kingdom come, in Christ and through the Holy Spirit. We are called to collaborate by serving the cause of justice and peace.
- Invite feedback on this illustration and its commentary (about 5 minutes).

Read and reflect

- Ask participants to read pages four and five. Follow the same process for reading and reflection that you used for the first pages.

Share it with others

- Read the reflection on slide 6 and/or the reflection(s) provided in the booklet. Use the same format for group discussion and sharing as you did for the previous pages.
- Use PowerPoint slide 7 to provide the group with a visual of a Scripture passage. Open your Bibles to Matthew 6:10b–11, and select a few verses to read aloud. How does this Scripture passage relate to what you have just read and discussed?
- Pause for a few moments of silence.

Pages six and seven

Personal experience

- Ask everyone to look at the heading on page six, "And forgive us our trespasses." Invite them to reflect on these questions: If God forgave you as you forgive others, how would you fare? What can you do to become more forgiving?

Read and reflect

- Again, follow the same process for reading and reflection on pages six and seven.

Share it with others

- Read the reflection on slide 8 and/or the reflection(s) provided in the booklet. Use the same format for group discussion and sharing.
- Use PowerPoint slide 9 to provide the group with a visual of a Scripture passage. Open your Bibles to Matthew 6:12–13, and select a few verses to read aloud. How does this Scripture passage relate to what you have just read and discussed?
- Pause for a few moments of silence, then ask the participants to look at the illustration on slide 10, which is the same as the one on these pages. Refer to the quote on the back cover. We Catholics are people of the living word of God, leading and guiding us in today's world. The Our Father is a summary of the Good News of Christ. We pray that God provide food not only for us, but also all those in need; that we may forgive and be forgiven; we have the strength to resist temptation and evil.

Exercise

- Invite the participants to sing a version of the Our Father together (e.g., the Gregorian chant) or a psalm to God, such as *For You Are My God*, by John Foley (OCP) or *Though the Mountains May Fall*, by Dan Schutte (OCP).

Take it home

- Before the end of the evening, ask the small groups to talk once more about how they plan to take home and live what they have learned. Refer to the reflections, and suggest they use them to help apply the core message of this booklet. Invite them to make concrete and realistic plans. Allow a few minutes for this discussion.

Conclusion

- Go to slide 11 and announce the time and place of the next gathering.
- Go to slide 12 and invite everyone to pray the closing prayer aloud. (You can make copies of the prayer, found on page 29 of this guide, or use the prayer of Blessed John XXIII on page 5.) You can, instead, invite the group to offer spontaneous prayer. You may also close the evening with the dismissal song on the CD.

Appendix I

Six intentional modules

Below are six shorter configurations of sessions for using *Growing Faith Project* over a two or three year period. When used in sequence, these six modules will result in a systematic and comprehensive presentation of the Catholic Faith. A planner is provided for your use in Appendix II.

1. Creation and Revelation	*Booklet*
What does your heart desire?	1
Where do you meet God?	2
How does God speak to us?	4
Do you believe?	5
How did God create the world?	8
How are we in God's image?	9
Why do people turn away from God?	10
What makes us free?	30

2. The Trinity and the Nature of God	*Booklet*
In whom do you believe?	6
What is the love of the Trinity?	7
Who guides and inspires you?	16
What happens at the end of life?	20
What is right and wrong and how do we know?	31
How does God speak to us in prayer?	46
What ever happened to grace?	35
What is prayer?	44

Appendix II

Index to the Catechism of the Catholic Church

Item	GF Booklet	Catechism #
Abortion	40	2270–2275
Adam and Eve, figurative language	10	390
Adultery	41	2380–2381
Agnosticism	37	2127–2128
Angels	9	328-336
Animals, the care of	42	2415–2418
Anointing	27	1499–1532
Anointing, the rite	27	1517–1519
Atheism	37	2123–2126
Authority	34	1897–1904
Baptism	23	1213–1274
Baptism, the rite	23	1229–1245
Beatitudes	30	1716–1717
Beauty	43	2500–2503
Bishops, ordination of	28	1555–1561
Bishops, successors to apostles	3	77–79
Blasphemy	37	2148
Boasting	43	2481
Capital punishment	40	2266–2267
Chastity, defined	41	2237–2347
Children, conceiving and bearing	41	2366–2379
Children, duties of	39	2214–2220

Item	GF Booklet	Catechism #
Christ, ascension of	15	659–664
Christ, Incarnation	11	461–463
Christ, judge of living and dead	15	668–679
Christ, life of	13	522–540
Christ, mystery of his life	13	512–515
Christ, only Son of God	11	441–451
Christ, passion of	14	557–623
Christ, Reign of God	13	541–556
Christ, resurrection of	15	638–655
Christ, the heart of faith	11	422–483
Church, and non-Christians	18	839–848
Church, body of Christ	17	787–796
Church, images of	17	751–757
Church, lay faithful	19	897–913
Church, marks of	18	811–865
Church, mystery of	17	770–776
Church, our need for	3	74–95
Church, people of God	17	781–786
Church, pope and bishops	19	880–896
Church, precepts of	36	2041–2043
Church, religious	19	914–933
Church, temple of Holy Spirit	17	797–801
Citizens, duties of	39	2238–2243
Common Good	34	1905–1917
Communion of Saints	20	946–953
Confession (see Reconciliation)		
Confidentiality	43	2488–2492
Confirmation	24	1285–1321
Confirmation, East and West	24	1290–1292
Confirmation, the rite	24	1293–130
Conscience	31	1776–1794
Covenant, Abraham	2	59–61
Covenant, Noah	2	56–58
Creation, mystery of	8	295–301
Cursing and swearing	37	2150–2155
Deacons, ordination of	28	1569–1571
Dead, respect for	40	2299–2301

Item	*GF Booklet*	*Catechism #*
Death, meaning of	20	1010–1014
Defense, using violence for	40	2263–2265
Deposit of faith	3	84
Divorce	41	2382–2386
Domestic church	29	1655–1658
Emotions and passions	31	1762–1770
Envy	42	2538–2540
Eucharist	25	1322–1419
Eucharist, presence of Christ	25	1373–1381
Eucharist, the Mass	25	1345–1355
Euthanasia	40	2276–2283
Evil, reality of	10	386–387
Evil, why does it exist?	8	309–314
Faith, implications of believing	6	222–227
Faith, our response to revelation	5	142–175
False witness and perjury	43	2476
Family life	39	2201–2233
Fornication	41	2353
Freedom, of humans	30	1730–1742
Gambling	42	2413
God, as Divine Love	6	218–221
God, as one	7	253
God, belief in	6	199–221
God, creator of all	8	279–294
God, Father and Mother	7	239
God, loves creation	8	302–308
God, name revealed	6	203–209
God, self-communication	2	51–6
God, the nature of	1	36–43
Gossip	43	2477–2479
Government, civil authority	39	2234–2246
Grace	35	1996–2011
Greed	42	2536
Growth in understanding	3	94
Health, respect for	40	2288–2291
Heaven	20	1023–1029
Hell	20	1033–1037

Item	GF Booklet	Catechism #
Holiness	35	2012–2016
Holy Orders	28	1533–1600
Holy Orders, the rite	28	1572–1574
Holy Spirit	16	683–741
Holy Spirit, gifts and fruits of	32	1830–1832
Holy Spirit, in the church	16	731–741
Holy Spirit, symbols of	16	694–701
Homicide	40	2268–2269
Homosexuality	41	2357–2359
Humans, desire for happiness	30	1718–1724
Humans, in the image of God	9	355–361
Humans, made for each other	9	371–373
Humans, partners in creation	10	374–379
Hunger for God	1	27–30
Icons and images of God	37	2129–2132
Idolatry	37	2112–2114
Incest	41	2388
Indulgences	26	1471–1479
Infallibility	19	888–892
Intercession, prayer of	45	2634–2636
Jesus, the name	11	430–435
Just wages	42	2434
Justice, among nations	42	2437–2442
Justice, economic	42	2426–2436
Kidnapping and torture	40	2297
Law, moral	35	1950–1974
Law, natural	35	1954–1960
Law, old and new	35	1961–1974
Liturgical seasons	22	1163–1178
Liturgy, meaning of	21	1069–1109
Liturgy, and culture	22	1204–1206
Liturgy, diverse rites	22	1200–1203
Living together without marriage	41	2390–2391
Lord's Prayer	48	2759–2865
Lust	41	2351
Lying	43	2482–2487
Magic	37	2115–2117

Item	GF Booklet	Catechism #
Prostitution	41	2355
Purgatory	20	1030–1032
Purity	41	2517–2527
Rape, act of violence	41	2356
Rash judgment	43	2477
Reconciliation	26	1420–1498
Reconciliation, many forms	26	1434–1439
Reconciliation, the rite	26	1450–1460
Religious freedom	37	2104–2109
Resurrection of the body	20	988–1004
Revelation, complete in Christ	2	65–67
Revelation, stages of	2	51–67
Revelation, transmission of	3	74–95
Sabbath	38	2168–2173
Sacraments, meaning of	21	1113–1130
Sacraments, signs and symbols	22	1145–1162
Sacrilege	37	2120
Satan	10	391–395
Scandal	40	2284–2287
Scientific research	40	2292–2296
Scripture	4	101–133
Sexual activity in marriage	41	2360–2365
Simony	37	2121–2122
Sin, defined	33	1849–1864
Sin, mortal and venial	33	1854–1864
Sin, what is it?	10	396–401
Sin, why God permits it	10	410–412
Slavery	42	2414
Social doctrine of the church	42	2419–2425
Social justice	34	1928–1938
Society, defined	34	1878–1885
Suicide	40	2280–2283
Suicide, mercy of God	40	2283
Sunday	38	2175–2188
Superstition	37	2111
Tempting God	37	2119
Ten Commandments, about	36	2052–2074

Appendix III

Annotated Resources

General Resources

- *General Directory for Catechesis* (Washington, DC: USCCB, 1998). This directory, called for at Vatican II in the Decree on the Pastoral Office of Bishops in article 44, was many years in development and is an extraordinary guide for all those in faith formation ministries.

- *General Directory for Catechesis in Plain English* (Bill Huebsch; Mystic, CT: Twenty-Third Publications, 2001). This is an article-by-article commentary and reflection on the original GDC and retains the article numbers so it is possible to use it as a pathway into the Directory.

- *Our Hearts Were Burning Within Us* (Washington, DC: USCCB, 1999). The US Bishops' plan for adult formation is presented in a powerful way in this document. A must-read for all in adult formation. It picks up where an earlier US Bishops' document, *Serving Life and Faith*, 1986, left off.

- *Leader's Guide to Our Hearts Were Burning Within Us* (USCCB, 2000). An extremely helpful tool in planning for adult faith formation at the parish level. The Guide includes within it a copy of the Bishops' pastoral letter. Filled with worksheets and helpful resources.

- *Nurturing Adult Faith: A Manual for Parish Leaders* (Kristina Krimm, Jane A. Pierron, and David M. Riley, editors; Washington, DC: NCCL, 2003). This excellent resource is a handbook for understanding adult faith formation. Packed with tidbits and pertinent outside resources. It gives many concrete, specific adult faith formation process details.

Whole Community Catechesis Resources

- *Generations of Faith Resource Manual: Lifelong Faith Formation for the Whole Parish Community* (John Roberto with Mariette Martineau; Mystic, CT: Twenty-Third Publications, 2005).

- *Handbook for Success in Whole Community Catechesis* (Bill Huebsch; Mystic, CT: Twenty-Third Publications, 2004).

- *Here Comes Everybody: Whole Community Catechesis in the Parish* (Leisa Anslinger; Mystic, CT: Twenty-Third Publications, 2004).

- *Heritage of Faith: A Framework for Whole Community Catechesis* (Jo McClure Rotunno; Mystic, CT: Twenty-Third Publications, 2004).

- *Increase Our Faith: Parish Prayer Services for Whole Community Catechesis* (David Haas; Mystic, CT: Twenty-Third Publications, 2004).

- *Rooted in Christ: A Complete Guide for Catechist Faith Formation* (Jeanne Wiest; Mystic, CT: Twenty-Third Publications, 2005).

- *Whole Community Liturgy: A Guide for Parish Leaders and Lay Ministers* (Nick Wagner; Mystic, CT: Twenty-Third Publications, 2005).

- *Whole Community Catechesis in Plain English* (Bill Huebsch; Mystic, CT: Twenty-Third Publications, 2002).

- *Whole Community Catechesis: A Pastor's Guide* (Bill Huebsch; Mystic, CT: Twenty-Third Publications, 2004).

Video/DVD Resources

- *Seven Key Principles of Whole Community Catechesis* (Bill Huebsch; Mystic, CT: Twenty-Third Publications, 2004).

Periodicals

- *RTJ: The Magazine for Catechist Formation* (Alison Berger, editor; Mystic, CT: Twenty-Third Publications).

- *Today's Parish* (Daniel Connors, editor; Mystic, CT: Twenty-Third Publications).